Six Ensemble Plays for Young Actors

East End Tales, Wan2tlk?,
Stuff I Buried in a Small Town, Sweetpeter,
The Playground, The Odyssey

East End Tales: a series of nine stories inspired by news articles from local papers in east London. Written in a heightened lyrical style, the tales range from short contemplations through to longer tales of domestic violence, the drudgery of part-time jobs, petty crime and high density living. They offer great scope for ensemble performance.
Age range: 11–20; **cast**: open to interpretation;
running time: 20–45 minutes

Wan2tlk?: a fast-paced introduction to how to survive as a teenager, exploring the craze of mobile phone culture, gangs, and the pressure to have whatever it takes to fit in, at whatever cost… Welcome to the nail-biting world of text-messaging known as thumb-culture.
Age range: 11–17; **cast**: 20+; **running time**: 60–90 minutes

Stuff I Buried in a Small Town: when seventeen-year-old Danny's life collides with Krissie after a bad first-date, his vicious attack threatens to determine the course of both their lives. Intertwining stories confront issues of peer pressure and addiction: together they highlight the importance of young people learning to trust their own values and beliefs so as to grow as individuals.
Age range: 14–25; **cast**: 20+; **running time**: 45–60 minutes

Sweetpeter: born in 1787 on a slave-ship and immediately murdered by his father who wants to spare him from a life of slavery, Sweetpeter is a mythical boy with seven lives. In this free-wheeling play that thrillingly blends movement, music and verse, Sweetpeter embarks on a roller-coaster journey travelling through time to be reunited with his father.

Age range: 11–25; **cast**: 6; **running time**: 75–90 minutes

The Playground: in the grim playground of her new primary school, Ola encounters the spirit of the ancient Copper Beech Tree and inspires a campaign to make the playground beautiful again. She discovers a secret garden but will she and the other pupils succeed in saving it from contractors, or will it serve as a reminder to Ola of the devastation wrought in her native Nigeria?

Age range: 5–15 years; **cast**: 20+; **running time**: 20–45 minutes

The Odyssey: an adaptation of Homer's epic poem dramatising Odysseus's quest to return with his men to his homeland after the fall of Troy. Along the way, the intervention of the gods, the great Cyclops, the Sirens and a host of other dangers must be overcome in this exhilarating play for a large cast.

Age range: 11–20; **cast**: 20+; **Running time**: 90–120 minutes

Six Ensemble Plays for Young Actors

East End Tales
Fin Kennedy

Wan2tlk?
Kevin Fegan

Stuff I Buried in a Small Town
Mike Bartlett

Sweetpeter
John Retallack and Usifu Jalloh

The Playground
Kay Adshead

The Odyssey
Hattie Naylor
(adapted from Homer)

introduced by

Paul Roseby

Methuen Drama

1 3 5 7 9 10 8 6 4 2

This collection first published in Great Britain in 2008 by Methuen Drama

Methuen Drama
A & C Black Publishers Limited
38 Soho Square
London W1D 3HB
www.acblack.com

ISBN: 978 1 408 10673 0
A CIP catalogue record for this book is available from the British Library

Typeset by SX Composing DTP, Rayleigh, Essex
Printed and bound in Great Britain by CPI Cox & Wyman, Reading, RG1 8EX

Caution

Contents

Foreword   vii

Introduction   ix

East End Tales   1

Wan2tlk?   37

Stuff I Buried in a Small Town   85

Sweetpeter   159

The Playground   223

The Odyssey   263

Foreword

Six Ensemble Plays for Young Actors is an anthology of work
written specifically for young people to perform. This
development – part of the Young People's Participatory
Theatre project* – came about in response to a widely held
belief that there is a lack of high quality work suitable for
young performers. Following a hunch that there was a
largely untapped resource of unpublished, infrequently
performed, dramatic writing lying forgotten on shelves or in
drawers, Arts Council England, in partnership with Methuen
Drama, launched an online survey for the public to suggest
plays for inclusion in an anthology. Nominations could be
made by the author/s, producer/director, performer or
audience member with the only proviso being that the play
needed to have been performed at least once but not
previously published. The work could be a commission,
collaboration or a script devised with or by young people.

The call out for scripts generated an extremely positive
response and was fantastically encouraging in the range and
quality of work we received for consideration. The process
for selection was rigorous and the final selection was arrived
at after months of deliberation, with consultation from
theatre professionals, young people, Arts Council England
staff and Methuen Drama editors.

We would like to thank the many people who have
helped bring this project to fruition, especially all those who
submitted plays, those who undertook the immense task of
reading and assessing all the scripts, the Arts Council
England YPPT Youth Council and publication steering
group, and in particular the final judging panel.

Sarah Lovell
YPPT Project Manager, Arts Council England

* The Young People's Participatory Theatre programme is a three-year
Department of Culture, Media and Sport funded initiative to develop youth and
participatory theatre in England for young people aged 11–25 years. The
definition of theatre within the scope of this project includes circus, street arts and
experimental theatre. The programme aims include: a commitment to increasing
young people's access to and participation in theatre; raising the profile and status
of participatory work, and positively addressing issues of quality.

Introduction

I suspect the majority of you picking up this publication will
be what is commonly known as 'young', and by that I mean
under the age of twenty-five. I take no credit for coming to
that somewhat obvious assumption, after all there's a clue in
the title *Six Ensemble Plays for Young Actors*. I do however think
there's a need to explain in this youth obsessed age why
there should be a collection of plays for young actors and as
I'm the one writing the introduction I will at least take credit
for that!

As Artistic Director of the National Youth Theatre of
Great Britain, I meet around 4,000 young people each year,
and this diverse company of talented young actors,
technicians, and designers are I think a fair representation of
Britain's youth. Some are disengaged totally from society
and from what it claims to offer a young person in way of
career opportunities, and some are the highest achievers in
the UK with a wealth of confidence and opportunity at their
disposal. One of our great challenges is to bridge that social
divide through the process of theatre making and the sheer
thrill of live ensemble performance, be that as a participant
or as a member of the audience. There is, though, another
challenge of equal importance and one that is more
poignant than ever before as we begin to define the 'iPod
generation' and what effect this is having on live
performance now and in the future.

The recent technical revolution has allowed our
mechanical portals of communication to shrink and become
very user friendly. One advantage of this is that it's allowed
us to live a life in detailed miniature: an intimate moment
with your iPod; a quick-fire text exchange; a snapshot on a
social networking site – all feeding into our new world of
what I call 'micro-drama'. However exciting, immediate
and accessible this new era may be, there is one potential
casualty: theatre, and along with it the ability to story tell in
front of a live audience. This might seem rather alarmist
and a bit of a middle-aged rant, but ensemble storytelling is
the oldest theatrical art form and when it's good it is still the

most exciting form of entertainment. If young people don't have an opportunity to take part in it and witness it for themselves then the genre is sentenced to a 'virtual' life in a remote corner of a museum marked deceased.

What is so fantastic as you read this anthology of new ensemble plays is the wealth of imaginative worlds they create and the subsequent challenge they bring to any performer, director and designer as to how best to portray these to an audience that might never have seen any theatre before. The NYT recently hosted a writing competition in conjunction with BBC Blast, and the short-listed writers came to our headquarters in North London for a master class hosted by writer Mark Ravenhill and director Natasha Betteridge. What was most telling, was the fact that the majority of the teenagers had never seen any live performance before and those that had said they preferred going to the cinema! Here lies your challenge. There's no question about having to compete with the blockbuster realism of cinema, but what you have in these six plays is an opportunity to create a piece of original theatre that should excite and engage an audience enough to make them want to go to the theatre again. No pressure, but the responsibility is yours!

My advice may sound obvious, but never forget your audience – after all this is why you do it. Staging one of these plays is about creating a good story, creating good young actors and creating new audiences. For me and I hope for you too, the importance and thrill of young people working together in theatre – be it on or off stage – cannot be emphasised enough as a production any one of these plays will illustrate so wonderfully.

The playwrights here all have impressive credentials as theatre makers and prove admirably that you don't have to *be* a young person to *write* for a young person! When given the challenge to do exactly that some writers are tempted to compromise a story line to suit the less experienced performer. I believe that is a mistake. From my experience a young person can be as sophisticated and as truthful a performer as the more seasoned world-weary one. No such compromise here then as each author has written for an intelligent, talented, young actor with no apologetic tone or soft-touch subject matter.

As much as I love ensemble plays, they can be guilty sometimes of style over content, but all six here have both in equal measure, with strong, content-rich subjects matched with bold theatrical style. They are also as diverse as they are challenging. The stark contemporary reality of racism in Mike Bartlett's *Stuff I Buried in a Small Town* contrasts with the fun surrealism of the world of caricatured mobile phone speak in Kevin Fegan's *Wan2tlk?*. In Fin Kennedy's *East End Tales* the hard hitting and part-bleak, part-comic context of the short stories is made even more compelling by their pure simplicity and lyrical language. Some poignant prose can also be found in *Sweetpeter* where the play's success stems from a cross-cultural collaboration between John Retallack and Usifu Jalloh. Here the historical struggle of slavery is told in a unique and moving way with equal doses of sweet and sour imagery. From the political we move to the spectacle of Kay Adshead's wonderfully inventive, high spirited *The Playground*: this is a feast of fun and deserves to be staged in every school playground. It is also a fantastic introduction to the trials and tribulations of site-specific performance for any young performer. The beauty here though is its potential to involve as many pupils as possible with the added benefit of transforming the normal shrill noise of a school playground into a more celebratory sound! The epic tale of Homer's *Odyssey* is also celebratory, not least because it is the world's first ever ensemble play along with *The Iliad*. Adapted by Hattie Naylor, this version has less reverential formality than the original and is a great welcome mat for any budding classicist. As you journey through this publication it is probably very fitting that *The Odyssey* is the last of the six plays given that the story is one of adventure and exploration. Naylor offers up many inventive solutions to staging such an epic, and wittily plays with scale and story much to the relief I would imagine of the play's audience.

Sometimes the danger of large cast productions with a myriad of characters is that the story can become unclear. All of these plays offer an exciting challenge to any director on how best to stage them. So having praised the writers, I feel I should now redress the balance and focus on the director's role of bringing the words to life. I've had the happy and privileged experience of working with writers such as Arnold Wesker, Rebecca Lenkiewicz and Tanika Gupta, and their input on how their work should be staged has been invaluable. However there comes a time in any rehearsal schedule when the writer needs to, and more importantly *should*, leave the room! Obviously as this publication does not come with the writer literally to hand, their footnotes and stage directions are key in supporting any director's vision, but they should not be taken as gospel.

In order to make any text come to life, it is important that the director thinks in pictures first so as to create the visual framework from which to support the text. I'm loath to commit my next point to paper, as all directors crave a healthy budget, but the reality of being given a fat budget when staging young ensemble productions is about as likely as seeing The Royal Opera House stage a production of *Annie: The Musical*. These plays do not command a big budget, just a simple idea. If anything, the lower the budget the more inventive you and your company have to be in creating those pictures, and the more involved your cast and audience will feel as a result. Wit and invention are often far more impressive than big sets. In other words be lateral not literal. Live music can also do more than just cover up any loose ends; it can and should enhance the theatre of storytelling. Even a simple underscore from a single instrument while the actors speak can create the necessary effect, but be careful that the words and music do not end up competing with each other. Balance is the key and is the core ethos of any ensemble company. It is not about pulling focus; it's about listening, about discipline, about being a team player. Those skills are the greatest things you can learn as a young actor and which is why ensemble performance must remain part of our theatrical language. I believe these plays will go a long way in helping that tradition thrive.

The National Youth Theatre has been thriving as an ensemble theatre company for fifty-two years now. It was the first youth theatre in the world and it seems remarkable to think how radical it was in 1956 to see a play solely with young people on stage. Half a century later, theatre for young people is commonplace but it can still make an impact, change lives and indeed be radical. I hope these plays will inspire you to take part, to entertain, and to take risks. Oh, and to take your iPod out and listen to a good story. So good luck! And in the words of one of the greatest writers of all time, *on your imaginary forces work . . .*'

Paul Roseby
Artistic Director, National Youth Theatre

East End Tales

Fin Kennedy

About the Author

Fin was born in Brighton and lives in London. He works full-time as a playwright and playwriting tutor.

Plays for adults include *Protection* (Soho Theatre, 2003) and *How to Disappear Completely and Never Be Found* (Sheffield Crucible, 2006), which won both the John Whiting Award and a Peter Brook Award. Plays for teenagers include *Locked In* and *We Are Shadows* (Half Moon Young People's Theatre, 2006 and 2007) and *Mehndi Night* (Mulberry School at the Edinburgh Festival, 2007).

Fin teaches playwriting in schools, and is a visiting lecturer at Goldsmiths College and Boston University.

www.finkennedy.co.uk

About the Play

East End Tales is a series of nine stories inspired by photos and news articles from local papers in east London. It was written as part of a Half Moon Young People's Theatre *Scriptworks* project for Mulberry School for Girls in Tower Hamlets, London (www.halfmoon.org.uk). The story ideas were developed by a group of Year 10 Bengali girls over a number of weeks through a mixture of improvisation and written exercises, under the guidance of co-tutors Julia Voce and myself. I then selected the best material, shaped it, expanded it and wrote it up into a lyrical style for performance by an ensemble.

East End Tales was first performed on Saturday 15 May 2004 at Half Moon Young People's Theatre by the group of girls from Mulberry School, E1. The production was directed by Julia Voce, designed by Ruth Finn, produced by Chris Elwell and Imogen Kinchin and supported by the staff of Half Moon and Mulberry School.

The play is suitable for performance by any group of young people with a good level of maturity. The stories range from short contemplations on the nature of east London, through to longer tales of domestic violence, the drudgery of low-skilled jobs, petty crime and high-density living. Although they were inspired by east London, most can be adapted to any inner city setting. The tales are written in a heightened lyrical style and laid out in what looks like verse, the idea being that there are no individual character 'parts', only an ensemble of narrators, playable by any combination of male or female cast members. Each new line indicates a new speaker. The tales could therefore be delivered by two narrators or twenty, with the lines dotted around the stage among a crowd. In this way the play is written to allow the performers explicitly to acknowledge and address the audience. There are no stage directions, allowing the director and designer free rein in how best to bring the stories to life.

What the tales all share is a sense of the storytellers as slightly detached observers of the world around them. This allows the performers to find their own characters for the storytellers, or indeed to play themselves. In the original performances this ranged from gossipy sisters jostling for position on a sofa, through to a pair of cynical pigeons sitting on a telegraph wire observing events below them. The tone is matter-of-fact, but also bitter-sweet and occasionally poignant.

Because each tale is self-contained, it is possible to pick and choose among them to create performances of varying length, without affecting the overall narrative.

Prologue

Yeah I get all sorts in here
Make a crust innit
Work all hours me
Got a baby on the way
Y'know how it is
So it'd be nice
If you could sort us out
Wiv a tip
Knoworramean?

So you leave early did ya?
Oh right
Yeah right
Oh shame that
Never mind
Yeah it's still early for me
I'll probly go back
Pick up more punters
Knoworramean?

Yeah I'm
Y'know
Whassit
Whassaword
Autumnal
No
Nocturnal
Yeah
Yeah thassit
Nocturnal
Sleep in the day
Come out at night
I reckon
That's when
Y'see the real East End
Shadowy
Knoworramean?

Yeah
Some people
Some people say the city sleeps at night
Bollocks
That's when it's most awake
Yeah I see a lot
Not all of it nice
People all over the place
In my face
I put my foot down sometimes
I ain't havin it
Y'gotta draw a line
Knoworramean?

Yeah I've lived here all me life
Round here's my whassaword?
Stompin ground
Thassit
My stompin ground
Round here
Stomp about an that
Hahahahaha
Knoworramean?

Yeah my family's from back East
Nah
Bangladesh mate
Serious
Y'know Pabna?
Near Dhaka
Sort of
Nah me neither
Only been once
An I was two
So I don't remember fuck all
I'm a Londoner me
Shit
Jumped a light there
Woops

Nah
It don't bother me really
I mean
Not really
Well it does a bit
I spose
If I fink about it
Which I don't
Be nice to see me gran an that
Now and then
I got a baby on the way
Did I tell ya?
Oh
Oh right
Which turnin then?
Eh?

East End Tales 1

If the East End was my friend
He'd be
A boy
Nearly a man
So eighteen
Maybe younger
Fit
Yeah, sporty
But fit sexy too
Spiky hair
Mixed race
Bit of stubble
But unemployed
You reckon?
Goes to college
Okay, so he has a future
Sort of
He'd rather play football
Wouldn't they all?
Or Playstation
Bor-ing
But he hates cigarettes
Which is a start
Cos his dad used to smoke
And his dad used to hit him
So they remind him of home
In a bad way
Memories
Cos it's in the past now
He moved out
Ages ago
Going it alone
Independent
Yeah, cool
Doesn't see them any more
Doesn't miss em neither

Nah
Cos he's hard
Can stick up for himself
Even the traffic stops for him when he crosses the road

East End Tales 2

If the East End was my friend
She'd be
A woman
Twenty-one
So young
Get lost, that's old!
She's bold
Cold
But warm on the inside
A business woman
But works to live, doesn't live to work
Wears one of those suits with shoulders out here
But hates it, feels silly
Drinks wine, not beer
She's happy
And healthy
She jogs round the park
But she's secretly lonely at home after dark
She watches the news but it makes her depressed
She waits for the weather, for the weathergirl's dress
She'd quite like world peace
So she's got a good heart
But if the trains ran on time that'd be a good start
But most of all she wants
She wants
She wants
More shoes!
A personal shopper!
To fall in love!
A romantic cruise!

She's crazy about this guy at work
But he takes drugs at the weekends
And only talks to her if she wears a low-cut top
At night, she dreams of rainclouds
And her pillow is wet when she wakes

East End Tales 3

If the East End was my friend
He'd be a man
Thirty-something
Jack of all trades
A bit of this
A bit of that
A bit of everything
One of life's jugglers
He acts like he's rich
But if he was then he'd spread it
He'll say 'Life's a bitch'
And then ask you for credit
He'll tell some crap joke
And then ask if you geddit
If you met in the pub
If you bought him a drink
He'd smile and say
'Yeah cheers, London Pride'
But if you ask about his past
He won't look you in the eye
He'll turn away, light a fag
And make some comment about the sky
'Looks like snow again dunnit'
But his past is where it's really snowing
Whitewashed
Silent
Ancient secrets
Frozen solid under the ice
For it's winter
Mid-winter

A long time ago
Where the body of a man lies covered in snow
If Jack were to talk
Which he doesn't as such
He'd say 'I don't remember much'
Just a fight in a pub that spilled outside
Some guy had insulted his London Pride
A blow to the cheek
A boot to the jaw
Till one of them just didn't move any more
You can see all of this if you look in Jack's eyes
The loudmouth routine is just a disguise
The crap jokes and laughter
Are merely a ploy
Cos under it all he's a lost little boy
At home on his own Jack cuddles the quilt
For this lost little boy
Is frozen with guilt

East End Tales 4

It was raining
Hard
On a Sunday
Exactly the day when it shouldn't
Mid-afternoon
Racing's on
While the swollen drops explode into the pavement
And crash off the walls of the estate

I had to go out
Dad wanted a pack of fags
And me too tired to put up a fight
'Twenty Regals love, cheers'
I sigh
And grab the umbrella
'Yeah keep the change and all'
All 10p of it, yeah thanks Dad

Outside on the street I see her for the first time
Standing there alone
Waiting to cross
Traffic thundering past
Rain pummelling down around her and bouncing off her
    head
Grey hair matted black with the wet

I go over
Offer the brolly
Try and keep the rain off her pensioner's trolley
You alright?
And she looks up slowly
Almost in pain
Has she been crying, or is it the rain?

And her eyes
Her eyes
These watery eyes
Pale blue
Like the sky
Or the ocean maybe
Ancient, but young
Like an elderly baby

Look, come under here
And she comes a bit nearer
I offer my arm
And as her fingers slip round my elbow
It's like she's made of old newspaper
Yesterday's stories that the rain might wash away

I grab her trolley
Put my hand up to the traffic
And we dodder across
Up the mini-mountain of the kerb and into the shop
Land of plenty
Plantains
And tinned veg

Inside, she hands me a note
Crushed soggy from her fist
A list
Her list
If you can call it that
'Bread' and 'beans'
Was all it said
Beans on toast is it? And she nods

I find the aisle
Bread
Beans
Beans
Bread
Half an hour's work for her
Takes me ten seconds

At the counter, she smiles
And extends an arm
Pats my jacket
Takes down some crisps
Hands me the packet

And in a voice
That voice
Cracking
From lack of use
Creaking open like an old old door
She says
She says
'Nobody's ever helped me before'

Back in the flat
I realise with a sag
I've forgotten Dad's fags
'Where the bloody hell have you been?'

But I go to my room and shut the door
All I can think about is beans on toast
Being lonely

Cold
And old

I eat my crisps
And look out the window at the rain

East End Tales 5

Fucking hell right, there's this woman lived next door
Yeah, number four
Well, family they were really
Yeah, a family I spose
If you can call them that
Not like happy families or whatever
No way
Not at all
They were fucked up
But anyway, this is about the woman
Yeah

Lived next door, her and new boyfriend
He's only been there about a month
She's got twins from the last one, two girls
Tiny
Cute
But pierced ears
Aged, like, two
You know the sort
Pink
Like baby pigs

So about a week after he moves in
Early evening
We're trying to watch the telly
And this big row starts
Next door
At number four
Don't think too much of it
Just a domestic

These things blow over
You know how it is

But then a plate breaks
Or a vase
Or a plant pot
Anyway, something big
And smashable
Being smashed
Huge crash!
Against the dividing wall between our house and theirs

Woman screams
Dad just turns the telly up doesn't he
Yeah
Asks what's for tea
But next night, it happens again

CRASH!
Bloody great heavy thing, breaking again
Against OUR wall
Even Mum's heard it this time
Comes through from the kitchen, hands covered in flour
'Did you hear that?'

And Dad's like
'Ignore it, none of our business'
Puts the volume back on, cranks it up

Only this time, it happens again
CRASH!!
Huge thing, making us jump
And a scream
My god
A muffled scream
A scream that just goes on for miles

And Mum's like 'Should we – ?'
And Dad goes: 'NO'
Turns the telly up even louder

Cos they're shouting now next door
At number four
Really howling at each other
And it's like animals
Yeah
Wild animals in the night

And then the babies start crying
Those two little girls

Dad puts the radio on, as well as the telly
Cranks it up
And Mum's like
'How can you hear anything with that bloody racket?'
And Dad's like
'Exactly'

None of our business, you see

Next night, it happens again
And the next
And the next
And the next
Fuck it's like living in a zoo
Where all the animals are seriously pissed off

The crashes against our wall are sounding lower
And duller
Solid
And thick
Less like a plate
And more like
I dunno
An elephant
Yeah
Or a baby pig

On the fifth night, in the midst of it all
CRASH!
Etcetera

Mum's like 'I can't take this any more, I've got to say
    something
You know, DO something'
And Dad's like, there
TV on full
And the radio
And the stereo
'None of our business!' he yells
Over Anne Robinson
You are the weakest link, goodbye

But before you know it, Mum's out the front
Down the path
Turning right
Banging the door
Of number four

The argument
STOPS
Like a car into a wall
Bam
Nothing

There's a silence
Then a creak
Then a few words exchanged
And before we know it Mum's back in the hall

Bloody hell, what an anti-climax
We wanted a scene like in 'Neighbours from Hell'
Channel Five 8 p.m.
All chainsawing each other's fences
And kicking each other's dogs
But there's nothing
Just Mum, looking glum
What did she say? What did she say?
'She said it's none of our business'

It seemed to stop for a bit after that
Couple of nights anyway

We watched 'Neighbours' and Dad watched 'Weakest Link'
And shouted at Anne Robinson in peace
And we almost forgot about number four
About next door
Maybe he just hit her more quietly
Or they'd run out of things to smash

Then
About a week later
And I'm in the caff on the main road getting chips and hot
    wings
And she's there
Sarah I think she was called
Or Sally
It was in the papers
Anyway she's there with her pram
At the counter
Buying a cup of tea to take away
And her face
That face
Swollen
Bleeding
Overcast
Like she'd lost a fight with a pane of glass

Somehow, like an idiot, I knock into her
And the Styrofoam cup cascades out of her hands
And a great fountain of hot tea yawns through the air
And showers the floor with brown

Oh no
Oh shit
This is it
She's gonna take it out on me
I stand and wait
And hesitate
Amidst a sea of tea

I'm
I'm

I'm
I'm sorry

But she doesn't scream, or hit me
Or scratch my face
Or threaten to kill my mother
She just looks sad, and feeling bad
I offer to get her another

At the counter, as it's being poured, I become aware
That my gob is somehow ten yards in front of my brain
And chattering out of control

We
We
We
We live next door to you

We
We
We
We hear things

She looks at me
Wearily
And for a horrible moment, it looks as if she might cry

She takes her tea
I pay 30p
She looks at me and says
'You're free'

'You're free' she says 'so live your life'

Strange I thought
Yeah strange it was
Doesn't really answer the question
But even stranger, I look down at the pram
And it's empty

And I want to ask where the twins are
The babies
The pierced pink piggies

But she's gone
Out the caff, down the road
Tiny figure
Scrawny
Slight
Stumbling on a paving slab
Then round the corner out of sight

That night
Next door
At number four
He killed her, in that tiny room
And all around her
Broken plates adorned her temporary tomb

At first no one realised what he'd done
He upped and left, went on the run
But the milk piled up and it wasn't long
Before we realised what was wrong

Mum cried when they took her away
Tiny thing, under a sheet
The twins too
Turned out, they'd died first
Neglect
The papers said
She'd been pushing an empty pram round
For weeks

Now Dad can watch TV in peace
Which must be nice
A nice relief
It was none of our business
So we closed our eyes
You are the weakest link
Goodbye

East End Tales 6

So I'm sitting behind the bar
Keeping myself to myself
Sipping at my orange juice
One pound sixty-five, cos the landlord's a tight bastard
And I'm trying not to be noticed
Which isn't hard
Waiting for my brother to finish work

It's 10.45 on a school night
So there's not many people in
But they're trickling down to the bar like puddles on a slope
Last orders, ordering their last
For that night at least

They're standing next to each other at the bar
And at first I think they must be related
Mother and son
Cos the resemblance is amazing
Dark skin
Strong chin
Well-kept nails
But hair's a mess
Friendly eyes
Wide nose
Caribbean
At a guess

But while she's all friendly
Tired
But warm
He's got this sneaky edge about him
Sly
Yeah
And behind his eyes, some sort of brewing storm

Anyway, they order separately
Avoid each other's gaze
And I realise they're total strangers

Funny
Yeah funny, I think
Go back to my juice
Hardly any left now, be gone in a minute
One sixty-five
Bastard
Innit

But then a scuffle makes me look up
Shit
Warm tired woman, turning back from the bar
Has knocked into hard sly man
Spilled his drink all down his front hasn't she
And he's well pissed off
You can see his mood
I won't repeat now what he said, but believe you me
It was fucking rude

And I'm sitting there, as frozen as me ice cubes
Heart in me mouth
Air crackling with static
People looking over
If there was music
Which there wasn't
It would've stopped

And I'm thinking
Hoping
Pleading
Praying
Reaching out with all my insides
Don't hit her!
Please don't hit her!
The whole pub can see you've had a bad day!
But don't you hit her!
Don't you dare hit her!

And the whole pub's holding their breath
Pints frozen in mid-air
Fag smoke hanging

Pulses banging
Terrified at what might come
Thinking the same
Like one big creature:
She looks like your fucking mum!

And I swear down
I swear on my life
And you've gotta believe me
There and then
In that room
The lights flickered
The lights flickered
And for one half of one second
We made something happen
We made something change

Cos behind the eyes
Of hard sly man
The storm
Evaporates
And when warm tired woman puts her hand on his arm
Sucks her teeth and says
'I guess that's my round then'
Something in him
I dunno
Melts
Yeah, melts
And he just goes
Yeah
Yeah alright then
Yeah

And everyone breathes out
Aaaaaaaah

But what was even better
Yeah amazing
After she's got him his new pint, all foaming with froth
Cos my poor trembling brother can't hold the glass straight

They go and sit down, and drink it together!
Serious!

And they talk
And they talk
And they talk
And even though they're way out of earshot
I don't need to hear
Cos I can tell
I can tell

He's
He's
He's
Telling her
Yeah telling her
About how his mum died
Yeah
In hospital
That's right
The night he was first arrested
And so he wasn't there at the end
And how that was the last time he cried
Yeah
And she looks like his mum
Yeah
But he wouldn't say that
No
Cos he'd be embarrassed
But she knows
Yeah, she knows

And then
And then
And then
She's saying about how her daughter's in America
At college
And she misses her like mad
And she hardly ever rings
But she's that age, you know how it is

Doesn't want Mum intruding
And anyway, ringing America's a rip-off innit

And then
And then
And then
He's remembering his own daughter
Who's only four
And in care
Cos her dad was busted for dealing
The day before she was born
And though he doesn't say it, warm tired lady knows
She knows
That his baby daughter was the last person he kissed

And they smile a bit
Just a bit
And drink their drinks
And one of them makes a joke
And they think about the shit day they've had
But how it's nice that it ended like this

I don't know how it ends
Cos I had to go
But in funny way I don't wanna know

Something happened in that room that night
It was only small
It was only slight

The lights seemed to flicker
Which I know sounds strange
But we made something happen
We made something change

East End Tales 7

Saturday evening, and we're about to close
I'm standing behind the counter
Facing the rusty old till

Straight ahead there's the aisle filled with food
My brother stacking the shelves

Bored
So bored
Wanna go home
Get changed
Go out
But Dad's got different ideas
We're staying open late
An experiment
Capturing the pisshead market
Apparently
And what a lovely bunch they are

Kerr-ching
Four ninety-nine please
Snuffles
Grunts
Hands over a fiver it looks like he's chewed

Kerr-ching
Three ninety-eight mate
Coughs
Sprays the counter with phlegm
Chucks some change down on top

The lady from the community centre
In for a late-night pack of Regals
Catches their eye

'What you lookin at Grandma?'
Looks away
The fear in her eyes all the more extreme
From recognition
A flicker of something
Panic
Horror
Something from her past
She knows their type
I give her a wink, and a discount on the fags

Next please

Kerr-ching
Seven forty-one
He looks at me
'How much?'
Seven forty-one please
'Fuck's sake'
The prices are all on the front mate, I say
YOU picked em up

He gives me that look again
Clenches one fist
Curls up his lip, like a dog that's pissed
I am SO not in the mood for this

When he speaks
It's quiet, in a threatening way
From the back of the throat
Goes 'What did you say?'

I'm not having this, so I take him to task
'If you need help adding up mate, you only need ask'

That doesn't seem to go down too well
My brother's looking over now, senses something brewing
While pissed-up dog goes red with rage
And tries to think of something to say
But he's none too clever at this time of night
All he can come up with is 'You little –'
And he stops
Cos I make him
With one of those looks

And without knowing where the courage comes from
Maybe tiredness
Maybe no longer caring
Maybe just years of biting my tongue
Of suddenly feeling cocky and young
I hear myself saying
Saying
Saying

'If you use the word PAKI
I will slam your pissed head
In this till
Do you understand?'

VOOM!
I have never seen my dad move so fast in his entire life
Or my brother
Or my mum
They're suddenly there, behind me at the till
A picture of family happiness
Domestic bliss
Cos we're smiling
Smiling
Smiling away
Smiling at pissed bulldog man
Happy families
Hooray

'That's seven forty-one please'
And without another word
He pays

I got to go home early that night
Dad showed me the door
And I don't work much in the shop any more

East End Tales 8

Jon and Michelle
Two people I know well
Types that is
But they're real enough
You might even have passed them
On the way in
You might not have noticed
They might've come in

Imagine
Imagine

Imagine
There's a clap of thunder
And suddenly you're in the wrong place
It's early
Eerie
Just before sunrise
And hailstones bombard the darkness

Straight ahead, through the blitz
You can just see the two of them
She's standing in this alley-way
A burrow between buildings
An urban lioness at the entrance to her lair
To you and me it's no man's land
A place to avoid after dark
A lawless tunnel in the gangland war
Full of ghosts
Death
And overflowing bins
But to Michelle, queen of the concrete jungle
This is where she feels at home

The hail piles up like icy gravel
But Michelle won't shift
Protected from this violence by a shield
The luck of the devil
Perhaps

Far away in the distance
Jon approaches
Solid
Dependable
The stones pinging from his helmet
A workhorse, joined the Force
Local boy come good
Works hard to safeguard
His local neighbourhood

But something is different today
This is an ordinary place you and me pass all the time
But today, there's an atmosphere
Tension
Something about to happen

Usually it's silent here
A quiet pocket
Away from the roar of the East End rocket
Usually, if pins were to drop
Even one or two
It would be like an elephant passing through

But not tonight

There's a buzz, a static
An eerie hum
And all of a sudden
You wanna run

Then we see it, and I nudge you
A split second too late

A streak of colour through the hail
A red baseball cap darting across the road

He's fast
Too fast
Even for our lioness
Our urban queen of con
A textbook bag snatch
Bam!
And he's gone

But guess where he's heading
Yeah
Towards Jon

A second
And then Michelle begins to scream
My God does she scream
It's like

Her life savings were in that bag
Or her baby
Or her sanity
Something she can't live without

Maybe it's just the pride
Of an urban lioness
Used to being the hunter
Not the hunted
Unimpressed

But there's another movement
In the middle distance now
Our workhorse has pricked up his ears
His copper's sense sees him coming
And with racehorse reflex
He's primed

Red baseball cap streaks up the road towards him
Like blood across tarmac
Arcing out from some wound in the street
He sees he's rumbled, tries to swerve
To dodge this bobby on the beat

But Jon's good
He's very good
It's not the man he's after
But the bag he's nicked you see
And as red cap goes flying past
He plucks the apple from the tree

A textbook bag snatch back
Which is quite hard to say

Your heart's racing, pulse is pounding
Can't believe what you've just seen
But remember
In the East End
Nothing's ever what it seems

Red cap's off
Round the corner

Wisely thinks he'll flee the scene
And Jon's left standing
A policeman with a handbag
Like some comedy routine

He trots over
Like the horse that won the race
Like the gentleman courtier
Hero of the piece
Saviour of the day
Graciously
Valiantly
Handing the queen
Her rescued royal property

The queen
Spits
Wipes her pits
And opens her Stepney gob
'I didn't need your fuckin 'elp
Now fuck off Policeman Plod!'

Our queen, it seems
Is not a fan of the Force

She turns
Spins on a stilettoed heel
Drilling one more hole into the pavement
Already she's burrowing into her handbag
Like an over-perfumed rat
Rooting out whatever treasure made her scream like that

But Jon
The peaceful workhorse of the street
Friendly bobby on the beat
Is going red as she retreats
He's losing it
His eyebrows twitch
The ingratitude
This little bitch

Like lightning, his arm shoots out
I nudge you and go 'Long arm of the law'
But you don't laugh cos this is serious
She's spinning round
Cracked red claws out, ready to scratch
And in her other arm, the open bag
Comes flying round in an arc
And almost in slow motion
A little silver packet
Wrapped tight
Flashing in the morning light
Helicopters through the air
Her precious treasure
Her worst nightmare

Speed, weed
Crack, smack
It's hard to tell from this far back
Whatever
It ain't legal
And it's lying at the policeman's feet
And he knows
Yeah he knows

She doesn't even give him time to blink
WHACK!
And he's staggering back!
This is why she rules this place!
This is why she's the fighter ace!
She does things you would think are mad!
Like punching policemen in the face!

Fair enough really
Yeah fair enough
Only thing to do
Under the circumstances
I spose
Would you have done it?
Yeah
Who knows?

Show's over look
Oh yeah
He's off
Manic
Like some crazy sport
But there ain't no point
She'll never be caught

Sun's coming up
Away to the east
Morning light
Awakens the beast

Just another hard day's night
Life in the day, the East End way
I nudge you and say
Cup of tea?
Yeah go on then
Chips?
I reckon so
Hot wings?
Yeah wicked
Come on then let's go

Let's go then
So we go
Slowly up the road
Leaving London
And its madnesses
In the street below

Epilogue

Nah mate I ain't pickin anyone else up
Sorry
Nah I'd love to
Really
But it's been a long night
Look it's not personal
You got a nice face
Nicer than some I see
I'm just knackered
Alright?

Look
D'ya mind takin yer hand
Off the
Off the thingy
It's just that
Yeah I can see that
I'm not feelin too well meself as it goes
Touch of mornin sickness I reckon
Nah
Didn't think you'd believe me

Where?
Bloody hell
You're a long way from home incha
Look though – sun's comin up
Tubes'll be startin any minute
You can walk
You'll be fine
The night's over
Safe

Nah look
Nah really
Nah I've gotta get home
Nah I've gotta rest up
Been drivin all night

I'm fucked
Nah put yer money away
Nah it don't matter how much
Nah it don't matter
Nah it don't
How much?
Fuck me
Alright
Hop in
Now
Where to boss?

Wan2tlk?

Kevin Fegan

About the Author

Kevin Fegan was born in Shirebrook, Derbyshire. He works full-time as a playwright and poet. He has written to commission over forty plays for a wide variety of theatres, several plays for BBC Radio 4 (including a 'Classic Serial' and a 'Woman's Hour' serial), a few short films and has worked as a storyline writer for *Coronation Street*. Kevin has published eight collections of poetry and edited several anthologies. He is a regular performer of his own poetry.

www.kevinfegan.co.uk

About the Play

Before writing the play, *Wan2tlk?*, I led a few workshops with self-selected pupils from New Heys Community School in Liverpool, in order to research themes, characters and ideas around the subject of mobile phones. In 2001, they were suddenly everywhere and in the hands of most teenagers. But were we any better at communicating with each other? Original music was commissioned from Liverpool composer Tom Moss, the play was directed by teachers from the school and performed by the pupils. Names of characters and locations may be changed to suit the needs of the performing group. For example, the song 'Allerton Boys, Allerton Girls' refers to the area of Allerton in Liverpool where New Heys School is. A new group might want to change 'Allerton' to another location appropriate to their area.

    Wan2tlk? was especially commissioned by Arts-in-Regeneration Speke and Garston, in Liverpool, in association with New Heys Community School. The play was first performed at the Everyman Theatre Liverpool, 12–14 July 2001.

Characters

Jade, *cyberchick: Mercedes' computer friend*
1st Moby, **2nd Moby**, **3rd Moby**, **4th Moby**, *mobile phones*
Cyberdudes Chorus, *Jade's mates*
Mercedes, *girl*
Mrs Dyson, *Mercedes' mother*
Gucchi, *leader of Allerton Boys*
Beemer, *Allerton Boy*
Diesel, *Allerton Boy*
Nike, *leader of Allerton Girls*
Cream, *Allerton Girl*
Chelsea, *Allerton Girl*
Allerton Boys Chorus
Allerton Girls Chorus
Alexander, *Mercedes' boyfriend*
1st Shoplifter
2nd Shoplifter
3rd Shoplifter
Shoplifters Chorus
Tetley, *Alex's dad, a security guard @ Tesco's*
Teenagers Chorus
Parents Chorus
Reebok, *Mercedes' dad*
Girls Chorus

Songs

'Beautiful People'
'Allerton Boys, Allerton Girls'
'Shoplifters' Song'
'Teenagers v. Parents Song'
'Wan2tlk'

Scene One

Cyberspace. A computer game. Enter cyberchick, **Jade**.

Jade Hi, I'm Jade.
Welcome to the cyber-arcade.
It's my pleasure to teach you
everything you need to know
to become a first-class 'babe'.
Like all great computer games
there's only one golden rule
you have to follow to survive your teenage:
two words, 'be cool'.
It's that easy.
Okay, so you can't all be a superstar like me,
not everyone has a body to die for like mine,
not everyone has this face, it's a shame;
but, hey, we can all aspire to be cool.
Just be yourself, that's all you have to do
and everything else will fall into place.
Don't worry, I'm here to help you.
There are four accessories you must acquire
before you can successfully aspire
to be a top babe.
Accessory No.1 – every girl needs a moby:

A selection of **Mobile Phones** *run on.*

Mobiles Pick me! Pick me! Pick me!

Jade Now, which one shall it be?

Mobiles Pick me! Pick me! Pick me!

Jade *deselects them, one at a time.*

Jade Avoid the building brick –
pick one for its good looks, not as a weapon.
Nothing too small – after all,
people should see you making fone calls.
No obvious posers and no looney choons –
'The Simpsons' is okay but not 'Clare de la Lune'.

Jade *chooses the most handsome* **Mobile** *and flirts with him.*

What a girl really needs is service:
a good strong voicemail,
one you can keep on standby,
a peak user with one-touch keys
and a full style pack,
a power charger, vibration alert
and ultra compact,
rollover and roaming
and total connectivity –
mmm, you'll do for me.

Jade *walks off, linking arms with her chosen* **Moby**.

Can you imagine life without a mobile?
It just wouldn't be worthwhile.

The other rejected **Mobiles** *are left to complain.*

1st Moby   They should upgrade their friends not us.

2nd Moby   I wish we could all be handsfree.

3rd Moby   Their talk is cheap, their conversation dull.

4th Moby   No one considers the poor moby.

Mobiles   Our lives in the palms of their hands,
the pay-as-you-go generation,
there's only one thing matters to them:
communication, communication, communication.

1st Moby   It's, who's got the biggest memory?

2nd Moby   And how many choons can you play?

3rd Moby   Trouble with people is they have too many
fascias.

4th Moby   How many messages can you send in one
day?

Mobiles   Our lives in the palms of their hands,
the pay-as-you-go generation,

there's only one thing matters to them:
communication, communication, communication.

1st Moby   All they want is an easy life.

2nd Moby   Talk the talk, walk the walk.

3rd Moby   Nothing real to say to each other.

4th Moby   Just talk, just talk, just talk.

Mobiles   Our lives in the palms of their hands,
the pay-as-you-go generation,
there's only one thing matters to them:
communication, communication, communication.

Exit **Mobiles**.

Jade   Accessory No. 2 – the right clothes:

A full costume rail is wheeled on.

always go for a designer label,
as expensive as possible,
doesn't matter if it's a fake, no one will know,
beg steal or borrow,
not yesterday's look or tomorrow's,
what matters is today:
is white the new black?
is blue the new grey?
And don't forget the underwear, girls,
when your bits feel well cared for,
you can take on the world.
Accessory No. 3 – the right mates:

Jade *is joined by the* **Cyberdudes**. *Song: 'The Beautiful People'.*

Cyberdudes   Cool and rude,
we're the Cyberdudes.
Let's hear it for the beautiful people:
we're havin' it funky
we're havin' it safe
we're havin' it sexy
we're havin' it straight.

Checkout the choons
checkout the dress code
checkout the dancing
à la mode.
Cool and rude,
we're the Cyberdudes.
No messin' in our funky dressin',
tops and t-shirts ironed and steamed,
we're havin' it clean,
no room for crusties.
Creases in our hankies
creases in our hair
creases in our jeans
creases in our underwear.
We're havin' it rich,
sophisticated,
we're havin' it stylish,
up-to-dated –
you gotta look like somebody famous.
Checkout the choons
checkout the dress code
checkout the dancing
à la mode.
Cool and rude,
we're the Cyberdudes.
Take you for a spin on the dance floor,
then you'll want more
and you can have more
'cause we're dancin'
'til the break of dawn,
yes we're dancin'
from the day we're born
'cause the dancin'
is a feel-good factor
and we're beautiful,
yes we're the people,
we're the beautiful,
the beautiful people.

Cool and rude,
we're the Cyberdudes.

Jade   Accessory No. 4 – a cool boyfriend:
now then, girls, this is a gender issue.
What you have to remember
is that the male of the species
is about as subtle as a twelve-pound hammer.
The art of being amorous
is to be glamorous.
Believe me, with your essential moby,
the right clothes and the right mates,
boys will be queuing up at your gate.
So be choosy.
Males are a potential source of money:
choose one who likes to spend
spend spend on his girlfriend.
Preferably one with a decent set of wheels
to take you out for romantic meals.

Jade *looks into the audience for a man. At the same time the face of* **Mercedes** *appears on a big screen.*

Jade   Let me see, somewhere around here there must be a half-decent male.

Mercedes   Hang on a minute, Jade, get real: that might work fine in cyberspace but out here in the real world, you've got no chance.

Jade   Who's that?

Mercedes   It's me, Mercedes, I'm the one playing the game, remember?

Jade   That's the trouble with interactive software, there's always somebody there with a joystick trying to spoil your fun. If you just played the game you might learn something.

Mercedes   You live in a computer, what can I possibly learn from you?

Jade   That's prejudice and you know it. You think you're better than me because I'm made of numbers and you're made of water with a bit of carbon thrown in for good measure.

Mercedes   I haven't got time to argue with a two-dimensional perfectionist, I'm late for school as it is.

Jade   That's it, don't bother to switch me off, I'm leaving.

Screen goes blank. **Jade** *leaves.*

Scene Two

Breakfast at the **Dysons***' house.*

Mrs Dyson   Where is that girl? (*Calling.*) Mercedes?

Mercedes (*arriving*)   Sorry, Mam, I was just switching off my computer.

Mrs Dyson   You should do your homework at night, not in the morning.

Mercedes   A bit of last-minute research, that's all.

Mrs Dyson   You're leaving yourself late.

Mercedes   It's only school.

Mrs Dyson   You used to like school, I don't know what's got into you.

Mercedes   Mam, can I have a new moby?

Mrs Dyson   You've got a phone.

Mercedes   That thing, it's embarrassing.

Mrs Dyson   It works, doesn't it?

Mercedes   Not if I let the bus run over it.

Mrs Dyson   Don't you dare, I paid good money for that phone.

Mercedes   Mam, it's two years old, it needs upgrading.

Mrs Dyson   And? You're fifteen years old but we don't upgrade you.

Mercedes   Dad'd buy me one.

Mrs Dyson   Don't start.

Mercedes   If he was here.

Mrs Dyson   Well, he's not here, is he?

Mercedes   No.

Mrs Dyson   Even when he was here, he was good for nothing.

Mercedes   That's not true.

Mrs Dyson   It was him who left us, remember?

Mercedes   You drove him away.

Mrs Dyson   That's not fair.

Mercedes   If you were a bit easier to live with, he wouldn't have left.

Mrs Dyson   You don't know the half of it.

Mercedes   Because you won't tell me.

Mrs Dyson   You think your dad's so perfect, well he's not.

Mercedes   Neither are you.

Mrs Dyson   I'm glad he's gone.

Mercedes   I wish I was living with him.

Mrs Dyson   Go on then, go to him. See for yourself if him and his fancy woman would have you. You'd be in for a bit of a shock, I can tell you.

Mercedes   You're jealous 'cause she's younger than you.

Mrs Dyson   Don't you dare speak to me like that. If your father really cared, he'd be phoning up asking to see you.

Mercedes   How can he? He doesn't know where we live.

Mrs Dyson   'Course he does. He wants nothing to do with us, he's made that very clear.

Mercedes   He phones me up on my moby.

Mrs Dyson   Does he really? Well then, you can ask him for a new phone, can't you?

Mercedes (*leaving*)   I will.

Mrs Dyson (*calling after her*)   And while you're at it, ask him for some new clothes and a school uniform and dinner-money and trainers and coats and everything else he doesn't pay for.

Scene Three

School. Song: 'Allerton Boys, Allerton Girls'.

Boys   On the streets of New Heys
you will find us cruisin',
young and cool and hard
we've got a lot to prove.

Girls   On the streets of New Heys
you will find us flirtin',
girl meets boy meets girl
we're in the mood for love.

Gucchi   The name's Gucchi, this is my crew.

Beemer *and* **Diesel**   He's in charge, we're the sidekicks.

Nike   The name's Nike, a girl with a point of view.

Cream *and* **Chelsea**   This is Cream and this is Chelsea.

Gucchi *and* **Nike**   You can have the image, adopt the style.

Beemer *and* **Diesel**   Create an impression and wear the smile.

Cream *and* **Chelsea**   You can shed the tears of a crocodile.

Boys *and* **Girls**   But you ain't gonna get that Valentine's kiss

without the right connections.

Boys   On the fone in New Heys
you will find us textin',
fun and rude and loud,
we've gotta lot to say.

Girls   We're the girls of New Heys,
you will find us sexy,
sending messages
and teasin' boys all day.

Gucchi   My girl's Nike, she is the perfect mate.

Beemer *and* **Diesel**   He's the king and we're the generals.

Nike   My boy's Gucchi and I like to make him wait.

Cream *and* **Chelsea**   She's the queen and don't we know it.

Gucchi *and* **Nike**   You can have the image, adopt the style.

Beemer *and* **Diesel**   Create an impression and wear the smile.

Cream *and* **Chelsea**   You can shed the tears of a crocodile.

Boys *and* **Girls**   But you ain't gonna get that Valentine's kiss

without the right connections.

Boys   On the fone in New Heys
you will find us textin',
fun and rude and loud,
we've gotta lot to say.

Girls   We're the girls of New Heys,
you will find us sexy,
sending messages
and teasin' boys all day.

*A new lad, **Alexander**, arrives at school. **Mercedes** is watching.*

Gucchi   Here y'are, boys, who's the new kid on the block?

Diesel   Hey kid, what's your name? How old are you?

Alexander   Alexander, I'm fourteen.

Boys (*mimicking*)   'Alexander, I'm fourteen'.

Alexander   Can I join your gang?

Beemer   Er, I don't think so. Look at you. Fourteen years old going on forty. Where did you get them clothes – Age Concern?

Gucchi   Hang on a minute, let's give the kid a chance.

Alex   Thanks.

Gucchi   If he can pass the special Valentine's Day challenge.

Alex   What do I have to do?

Gucchi   You have to trap off with one of them girls over there.

Alex   They might not like me.

Gucchi   Don't be daft, they're gagging for it. Go on, ask one of them out, if you dare.

Alex *approaches the girls.*

Gucchi   They'll eat him for breakfast.

Alex   Excuse me, erm, I hope you don't mind, but, I was wondering, if, erm, oh hell, I don't know how to say this.

Nike   Spit it out.

Cream   He's blushing.

Chelsea   Arhh.

Nike   Get on with it, we can't wait around all day for your balls to drop.

Alex   Would one of you like to go out with me? (*Silence.*) On a date. (*Silence.*) We could just pretend, if you like, as long as it was in front of my mates.

Girls laugh.

Nike   I don't think so.

Alex *returns to boys' laughter.*

Gucchi   Try the old fogies' home next door, Alexander, you might have better luck there.

Alex's *mobile rings. It is a very uncool tune.* **Alex** *moves downstage away from them. Boys and girls laugh and exit.* **Mercedes** *appears downstage opposite with her mobile. A text message scrolls on the big screen:*

'*don't listen 2 them, they're a bunch of losers*'.

Alex types in his reply. Their text conversation appears on the screen:

'*can u c me?*'
'*of course*'
'*where r u? who r u?*'
'*i'm your girlfriend stupid*'
'*r u? gr8. when can we meet?*'
'*2nite. Tescos 7pm. b there*'
'*it's a date*'
'*remember, Alex, sex is like pringles: once u pop u just can't stop!*'

Alex   (*suddenly ultra cool*)   Wow! Boss news, I've got me a
    girlfriend!
Safe, sound, sorted.
Who'd 'ave thought it?
Me, Alex,
this close to sex.
I bet she's drop-dead gorgeous,
into bondage and orgies.
She must really fancy me.

Who can blame her?
I'm handsome, I'm witty.
Oh shit, what am I gonna wear?
Look at the state of me hair,
I can't go out like this,
She'll think I'm taking the –
I need some advice.
Who do I know that's nice?
Who do I know that's female?
Me sister? No.
Me mam? No. That's just too sad.
I know, I'll ask me dad.

Exit **Alex**.

Mercedes   Wish me dad would get in touch. Not even so
much as a text message. I'm not going on a date with this
ridiculous fone – 'moby dick' Jade calls it, it's like a building
brick. Well if me mam won't buy me one and Dad doesn't
exist any more, I'll just have to nick one, won't I? I'll go
down Tesco's early and rob one of them new Nokias, slip
my own sim card in and I'm away.

Exit **Mercedes**.

Scene Four

Tesco's. **Shoplifters** *wheeling their way through the aisles, helping
themselves to goods. A security guard,* **Tetley**, *is oblivious to their
thieving.* **Mercedes** *joints them to rob a new mobile. Song:
'Shoplifters' Song'.*

1st Shoplifter   To pay for your goods is the height of folly,
life as a thief is terribly jolly,
drifting down aisles with our shopping trollies,
filling them up with sweets and ice-lollies.

Chorus of Shoplifters
No time to stop
'cause it's shop 'til we drop,

everything's free
for the career thief,
why pay for your gifts?
It's much cheaper to shoplift.

2nd Shoplifter   Rows and rows of goodies and clothes,
all for the taking at your local Tesco's,
push your luck as far as it goes,
I think I'll have these, no I think I'll have those.

Tetley   I stand by the door
guarding the store,
watching for trouble,
upholding the law.
As everyone knows
there are people at Tesco's
who prefer not to pay
their own way in this world,
there are those who will steal
anything they can,
girl or boy, woman or man,
well, it's my job to catch them.

3rd Shoplifter   Biscuits and tea, chesse puffs and kiwi
all taste nicer when you get them for free,
egg fried rice, leg of lamb cut-price,
no need to worry which flavour curry,
we're all in a hurry
for faster foods, pasta and pot-noodles,
diet coke and artichokes,
a right turn here for chicken tikka masala
then a left at the cakes to the ice-cream parlour,
everything's within reach so grab one of each,
toys and clothes, music and videos,
custard and mustard,
tissues and booze –

Mercedes   And mobile fones,
without the need for a bank-loan,
I'll take this one please.

Chorus   No time to stop
'cause it's shop 'til we drop,
everything's free
for the career thief,
why pay for your gifts?
It's much cheaper to shoplift.

Tetley   I stand by the door
guarding the store,
watching for trouble,
upholding the law.
As everyone knows
there are people at Tesco's
who prefer not to pay
their own way in this world,
there are those who will steal
anything they can,
girl or boy, woman or man,
well, it's my job to catch them.

Alex *arrives for his date and greets his dad,* **Tetley**, *the security guard.*

Alex   Oh, hi Dad, busy?

Tetley   Very quiet tonight, son, nothing much happening. You're looking a bit pukka, what you up to?

Alex   Dad, I've got a girlfriend.

Tetley   Good for you, son, what's her name?

Alex   Dunno.

Tetley   Dunno? What sort of name's that?

Alex   I've not met her yet.

Tetley   What sort of girlfriend's that?

Alex   I'm meeting her tonight.

Tetley   At Tesco's?

Alex   She should be here any minute. I wondered if you'd got any hot tips for me, Dad?

Tetley   Yeah, tuck your shirt in. Here, you can borrow my tie.

Alex   Thanks, Dad.

Mercedes *emerges from the shop and takes* **Alex** *to one side.*

Mercedes   Who's your mate, Alex?

Alex   That's me dad. Are you my date?

Mercedes   Your dad's security?

Alex   Yeah, cool uniform, innit? Shall I introduce you? Wait a minute, I don't know your name?

Mercedes   Another time, let's go. The name's Mercedes.

Alex   Built to last.

Mercedes   Alex, I've heard it before.

Alex   Sorry. Wow, that's a cool fone.

Mercedes   Do you like it? I've just bought it.

Alex   Let me show it my dad. See if he'll buy me one.

Mercedes   No, I don't think so.

Alex   Did your dad give you the money?

Mercedes   Yeah.

Alex   You must have a cool dad. My dad's really sensible.

Mercedes   My dad's a bit wild; but he really loves me.

Alex   You can tell.

Mercedes   He's always sending me mad text messages.

Alex   My dad's opened a savings account for me.

Mercedes   Why? What is there to save for?

Alex   Dunno. He says I can have the money when I'm twenty 'cause then I won't be a teenager any more and I'll know what to do with it.

Mercedes   Parents are weird.

Alex   Thanks for, you know, earlier at school.

Mercedes   I don't know why you wanna join Gucchi and his crew.

Alex   I thought I might, you know, find a girlfriend if I teamed up with them.

Mercedes   They're like dogs chasing cars, they have no idea how to catch girls.

Alex   Did you get any Valentine's cards?

Mercedes   No. Don't want none.

Alex   Oh. I bought you this. (*He hands her a card.*) Tear it up if you like.

Mercedes (*reading*)   'Sex is evil,
sex is a sin,
sins are forgiven
so get stuck in!'

Alex   Sorry, I was just picking up on your text message about Pringles.

Mercedes   That was a joke.

Alex   What's the difference between a woman and a supermarket trolley? A trolley has a mind of its own.

Mercedes   That is a crap joke.

Alex   Sorry.

Mercedes   Where'd you get it from – a Christmas cracker?

Alex   Me dad told it me.

Mercedes   A little tip, Alex. Don't use jokes by parents or teachers or any adults for that matter.

Alex   Sorry.

Mercedes   And stop saying 'sorry' all the time.

Alex   Sor – okay.

Mercedes   Why are parents and seagulls alike? You should never look up to either of them.

Alex   I like you.

Mercedes   You don't have to play games now, I'm not like Nike and the rest of them.

Alex   No, I mean it, I really like you.

They move closer to kiss but are interrupted by **Nike** *and her posse.*

Nike   What's going on here, then? Look at the pair of lovebirds, eh girls?

Cream   Trapping off with the new boy again, Mercedes?

Mercedes   Shut up.

Chelsea (*to* **Alex**)   She likes the taste of new blood.

Nike   You wanna watch her, Alex, she's a right vampire when she gets going.

Mercedes   Look who's talkin'.

Alex   You're only jealous of her.

Nike   Yeah, right, I really want to make it with a spotty little oick like you. Come on girls, before she gets her 'daddy' on to us.

They leave, laughing

Alex   What does she mean by that?

Mercedes   Nothing. She's being a bitch. Thanks.

Alex   What for?

Mercedes   Stickin' up for us.

Alex   Is it true?

Mercedes   What?

Alex   That you trap off with every new kid at school?

Mercedes   Go ahead, take their side, see if I care, you're just like the rest of them. (*She leaves.*)

Alex   Don't go. I'm sorry, I didn't mean –

His mobile rings. A message appears on the big screen. There is the image of a revolver followed by the words:

'*u r the weakest link. We know where u live*'.

Alex *texts back. The conversation scrolls on the screen.*

'*who is this? leave me alone*'
'*Alex, you puff, have you done it with her yet? everyone else has. Gucchi.*'
'*course. I did it with her lots of times*'

Alex *looks up at what he's sent and panics.*

Alex   What have I done? I shouldn't have wrote that.

He switches off his phone and runs away.

Scene Five

Cyber-arcade. Enter **Jade**. **Mercedes** *appears on the big screen.*

Jade   Hey, Mercedes, my main woman.

Mercedes   Hiya, Jade.

Jade   Where you been? What's buggin' you? I thought you'd pulled the plug on the modem. A girl gets lonely here in the cyber-arcade.

Mercedes   I thought you were too cool to feel lonesome.

Jade   Yeah, well, that's in front of the other guys. You look like you caught a virus?

Mercedes It's nothing.

Jade If it's nothing, it must be boys? Or rather, a boy?

Mercedes There is a boy – Alex.

Jade Good for you, it's long overdue. Tell me all.

Mercedes Alex isn't the problem. He's a bit daft but he's honest enough. He wouldn't do anything to hurt me.

Jade Believe me, they haven't invented the male who isn't trouble for us females.

Mercedes It's me dad.

Jade That's where being a cyberchick is a definite advantage – no mam, no dad. Can't for the life of me understand why you people bother with them?

Mercedes Can you help me find him?

Jade Are you sure about this? You've already got one parent telling you what to do, do you really want another?

Mercedes Jade, I think you're a chip missing on the family values front.

Jade You saying I'm emotionally retarded?

Mercedes Erm, yes.

Jade Thanks very much. What I lack in family values, I make up for in fun.

Mercedes Well? Can you help me or not?

Jade Easy. Input all the data you have on your dad, I'll find him.

Mercedes Thanks, Jade, you're a star.

Mercedes *disappears from the screen.*

Jade I worry about that girl,
she goes around carrying the world

on her shoulders.
Trouble is, no one's ever told her
life is supposed to be fun,
especially when you're young.
Girls and boys
get out there and enjoy your teens,
it's a laugh, it's a scream,
it's only obscene
if you waste it.
Let's face it, the only thing sadder
than a grown-up trying to act like a teenager,
is a teenager trying to be grown up.
Makes me wanna throw up.

Scene Six

Dysons' house.

Mercedes   You look tired, Mam.

Mrs Dyson   I am tired. If you did a bit more around the house it might help , instead of leaving everything for me to do.

Mercedes   I've tidied my bedroom.

Mrs Dyson   Hallelujah!

Mercedes   Put your feet up, I'll make you a brew.

Mrs Dyson   What you up to?

Mercedes   Nothing. You're so suspicious.

Mrs Dyson   Years of practice. I could do with a holiday.

Mercedes   Why don't you?

Mrs Dyson   I can't afford for the both of us –

Mercedes   Go on your own. I'll be all right.

Mrs Dyson   I'm not leaving you.

Mercedes I could stay with me dad.

Mrs Dyson No.

Mercedes Why not? At least tell me where he lives?

Mrs Dyson He knows where to find you.

Mercedes I know he's in Wales – which town is it?

Mrs Dyson I don't want you running away down there.

Mercedes I won't, I promise. Just tell me which town?

Mrs Dyson He's not in Wales, he's on the Wirral: New Brighton. I don't know the address.

Mercedes You deserve a holiday, Mam. I could always stay with a mate.

Mrs Dyson (*noticing her new phone*) What's that?

Mercedes It's not mine.

Mrs Dyson Where'd you get that phone?

Mercedes I borrowed it, off Alex.

Mrs Dyson Who's she?

Mercedes It's a boy.

Mrs Dyson Boyfriend?

Mercedes Yeah, I suppose.

Mrs Dyson You'd better be telling me the truth.

Mercedes Ask him. His dad's a security guard at Tesco's.

Mrs Dyson So what? It's not him I'm worried about, it's you.

Mercedes Mam, I've had boyfriends since I was three at nursery.

Mrs Dyson Is it serious?

Mercedes   Oh yeah, we're gonna elope to Australia next week and live on *Neighbours*.

Mrs Dyson   I don't know what you get up to behind my back.

Mercedes   Mam, I'm not sleeping with him.

Mrs Dyson   I should hope not; you're not sixteen yet.

Mercedes   Didn't stop you and Dad.

Mrs Dyson   Who's told you that?

Mercedes   No one. I just guessed.

Mrs Dyson   Well, you guessed wrong.

Mercedes   Yeah, Mam, whatever.

Mrs Dyson   You shouldn't be quizzing your own mother about those things.

Mercedes   Who else is there to ask?

Mrs Dyson   Maybe it's time we had a talk.

Mercedes   It's a bit late for the biology lesson, Mother.

Mrs Dyson   I'm talking about relationships.

Mercedes   What can you teach me – you failed.

Mrs Dyson   That is so cruel. (*Tearful.*) I am not a failure.

Mercedes   I'm sorry, Mam. I didn't mean that. You've done your best, at least you've stood by me.

Mrs Dyson   Your dad'll soon realise how much he misses you.

Mercedes   Too late. It's too late.

They hug.

Scene Seven

*School. This time, **Alex** is standing with the boys. As **Mercedes** enters, the girls shadow her. She ignores them and approaches **Alex**.*

Mercedes   You comin', Alex?

Boys and girls laugh.

Alex   I'm, erm, hangin' out with the lads tonight.

Gucchi   Get stuck in, Alex, you can always text us again with your progress.

Mercedes   What's he saying?

Alex   I can't see me bird when I'm with me mates.

Mercedes   What did you just call me?

Gucchi   Did he not show you his little message?

Nike   Whereabouts did you do it, Mercedes? At the back of Tesco's in the car park?

Cream   Among the fruit and veg?

Chelsea   Down by the spicy sauces?

Gucchi   Alex, show Mercedes what you sent us? He was so proud of his latest conquest, weren't you Alex?

Mercedes   How could you?

Mercedes *storms off.* **Alex** *chases after her.*

Scene Eight

*At Tesco's. **Alex** is looking for **Mercedes** but runs into his dad.*

Alex   Dad, have you seen Mercedes?

Tetley   I need to talk to you about that young lady.

Alex   Later, I have to find her.

Tetley   This won't wait. Come with me.

Alex   What's happened?

Tetley *escorts* **Alex** *to a DVD recorder and inserts a disc.*

Tetley   I want you to watch this.

Alex   What is it?

Tetley   Just watch it.

On the big screen recorded CCTV footage appears of **Mercedes** *shoplifting her phone the day before.*

Tetley   It is her, isn't it?

Alex   Yes.

Tetley   She's in big trouble.

Alex   What you gonna do?

Tetley   What can I do? She's robbed from the store, I'll have to report her to the police.

Alex   She'll be arrested.

Tetley   Serve her right, might teach her a lesson.

Alex   You can't. Don't report her, Dad, please? She's my girlfriend.

Tetley   I don't have any choice. My job's on the line here.

Alex   Does anyone else have a copy of the disc?

Tetley   No.

Alex   You could mislay it.

Tetley   Alex, I'm surprised at you. I thought you were more responsible than that.

Alex   Don't tell the police.

Tetley   She'll do it again. I can't let her off scott-free.

Alex   Go and see her mam, give her the disc; let her deal with it.

Tetley   I don't know about that.

Alex   Please, Dad, for my sake, if not hers.

Tetley   I'm making no promises. If Mrs Dyson doesn't deal with the matter satisfactorily, I'll have to report it. I shouldn't be doing this.

Alex   Thanks, Dad, I'll come with you.

Tetley   No. You go home, I'll sort this out, it's my job.

Scene Nine

Dysons' house. **Mercedes** *is in her bedroom in conversation with* **Jade** *who appears on the big screen this time. Elsewhere* **Mrs Dyson** *answers the door. It is* **Tetley**. *We don't hear what's said but she invites him inside.*

Mercedes   I hate him.

Jade   That's lads for you.

Mercedes   I hate boys. They're such cowards when it comes to their feelings.

Jade   How many lads does it take to screw in a lightbulb? Ten. One to screw it in and the other nine to brag about it.

Mercedes   I thought Alex was different. He called me his 'bird'.

Jade   Girls are only called birds because of the worms they pick up.

Mercedes   How could he lie about me sleeping with him?

Jade   Men are like computers: they're always trying to solve problems when they usually are the problem.

Mercedes   I really thought we had a good thing going between us. We could talk to each other.

Jade   Why does it take millions of sperm to fertilise one egg? 'Cos not one of them will stop and ask for directions.

Mercedes   I wouldn't have him back now if he crawled on his hands and knees.

Mrs Dyson *and* **Tetley** *sit down to view the disc. We don't hear their conversation.*

Jade   Little boy crying in the street. Policeman asks him 'What's wrong?' 'I've lost me dad,' says the boy. 'What's he like?' says the policeman. 'Beer, fags and women,' says the little boy.

Mercedes   Me dad's the same – what is it with fellas?

Jade   I've got an address for you. And a telephone number.

Mercedes   You've found me dad? Why didn't you say?

Jade   You never asked. I was trying to cheer you up.

Mercedes   How did you find him?

Jade   Mercedes, I am a top-of-the-range cyberchick with full-on intellect – and very sexy with it.

Mercedes   You're amazin'.

Jade   That as well.

Mrs Dyson *and* **Tetley** *have finished watching the recording.*

Mrs Dyson   I don't know what to say. I feel so ashamed.

Tetley   Would you like me to leave you alone with your daughter, Mrs Dyson?

Mrs Dyson   No, please stay. I'll fetch her. (*Calling.*) Mercedes, I want you down here straight away.

Jade *disappears from the screen.* **Mercedes** *goes to her mum.*

Mrs Dyson   This is Alex's dad.

Mercedes   I know who he is – what's he doing here?

Mrs Dyson   You told me that phone belonged to Alex?

Mercedes   So I lied.

Mrs Dyson   You're not only a liar, my girl, you're a thief.

Mercedes   You what?

Mrs Dyson   Don't try and deny it. This gentleman has a recording of you stealing that phone.

Mercedes   I suppose Alex has put you up to this?

Tetley   Quite the opposite. Alex persuaded me to show it to your mum rather than report it to the police.

Mrs Dyson   The man is doing you a favour.

Mercedes   Do what you want.

Mrs Dyson   How can you say that? We need assurances this will never happen again or I'll take the disc to the police myself.

Mercedes   You would and all, wouldn't you? Shop your own daughter.

Mrs Dyson   If I thought it would stop you thieving – what's got into you?

Mercedes   I don't have to sit and listen to this.

Mrs Dyson   You stay there. I've not finished with you yet.

Mercedes   I've finished with you. I'm out of here.

Mrs Dyson   Get back here, young lady.

Mercedes *legs it.*

Tetley   Do you want me to go after her?

Mrs Dyson   There's no point. She'll be back when she's calmed down. What can you do with them when they're like that?

Tetley   I have my own problems with Alex.

Mrs Dyson   I do appreciate you giving her a second chance, even if she doesn't deserve it.

Tetley   She might have gone to see Alex?

Mrs Dyson   Sounds like they've fallen out.

Tetley   Look, Mrs Dyson, here's my mobile number. Give me a call if I can be of any help or if you just want a friendly shoulder to cry on.

Mrs Dyson   You've been a great help already. Thanks. It's not easy when you're on your own.

Tetley   I know, I'm in the same boat.

Mrs Dyson   I'm sorry, I didn't realise –

Tetley   His mum died when he was ten years old.

Mrs Dyson   That must have been awful for you both.

Tetley   I've just about got over it now. I'm not so sure about Alex.

Mrs Dyson   You'll have to call around another time, in more pleasant circumstances. When Alex and Mercedes have made up, bring him over, I'll cook us a meal.

Tetley   I might take you up on that. Listen, I won't keep you. I'm sorry to be the bearer of bad news; but, hopefully, it'll turn out all right?

Mrs Dyson   I'm sure it will. Good night.

Tetley   Night then.

Scene Ten

On the big screen is a pre-recording of teenagers' attitudes towards their parents. Enter **Mercedes** *and a* **Chorus of Teenagers** *as the recording finishes and is replaced by another one of* **Mercedes'** *dad,* **Reebok***, in his living room. It is filmed as if* **Mercedes** *is looking in through his window. Song: 'Teenagers v. Parents'.*

Mercedes   That's my dad in there,
sitting in his armchair
with a new family, a new wife,
he's getting on with his life.
No room for me
or my melancholy,
he's moved on a chapter, lost the plot,
I'm the child he forgot.

Teenagers' Chorus   Why do we bother with mams and
    dads
when all they do is make us feel small?
Do they forget so soon what it is to be young?
Do they have no memories at all?
What do you do when your dad's gone mad?
When your mam stands by so helpless?
Where do you go to find a superhero
When the adults refuse to help us?

Recording of **Reebok** *in his living room is replaced by a pre-recording of parents' attitudes towards teenagers. Enter* **Reebok** *and a* **Chorus** *of* **Parents** *opposite the teenagers.*

Reebok   Somewhere out there is my daughter.
If blood is thicker than water
I should go out and search, in the rain,
become her father again.
I can't believe
I've let her be deceived,
So why don't I phone her,
tell her I love her,
I made a mistake,

I'm the dad she must hate.

Parents' Chorus   Why do we bother with kids at all
When what they do brings heartache and pain?
Do they not see how hard it is for mams and dads?
Do they know how great is our shame?
What do you do when your child goes missing
When you can't help thinking the worst?
Where do we go to help our children to grow
When the children blame us for divorce?

As song ends, **Mercedes** *leaves.* **Reebok** *calls after her but she is lost in the crowd.*

Scene Eleven

Mercedes *meets* **Alex** *and tries to avoid him.*

Alex   Don't run away, please, I need to talk.

Mercedes   What's up? Your new mates dumped you?

Alex   I was bang out of order, I'm sorry.

Mercedes   Forget it, Alex, it's over.

Alex   I can't forget you.

Mercedes   You don't wanna know me, I'm trouble.

Alex   I tried to help.

Mercedes   You sent your dad round to my house.

Alex   To stop him going to the police, I did you a favour.

Mercedes   Thanks for nothing. You lied about me to your mates.

Alex   You lied to me about your dad.

Mercedes   Yeah well, I haven't got a dad any more. As far as I'm concerned he doesn't exist.

Alex At least your dad's alive; you shouldn't take that for granted.

Mercedes I'm sorry, I heard about your mam, you should have told me.

Alex It was a long time ago.

Mercedes It was really insensitive of me.

Alex How could you rob from my dad's store?

Mercedes I didn't know your dad worked there, did I?

Alex He says if you give back the fone, he won't press charges.

Mercedes He can have it. Here.

(*She hands the phone to him.*)

Alex He's given your mam the disc; but don't say anything to anyone, he could get the sack.

Mercedes He's all right your dad, isn't he?

Alex He won't let you off next time.

Mercedes There won't be a next time – well, not from your dad anyway.

Alex I don't know how you can joke about it?

Mercedes Why not? It's a laugh.

Alex Why do you want to get into trouble?

Mercedes I don't care.

Alex I care about you.

Mercedes Why?

Alex I like you. Look, can we start again?

Mercedes I dunno.

Her phone rings. She takes it off **Alex**. *There is a message which appears on the big screen:*

'hi it's dad. sorry not been in touch. wan2tlk?'

Mercedes   It's him, it's me dad, he's text me. He's not disowned me, he does care, I told you.

Alex   I thought you just said –

Mercedes   Never mind what I said, I have to text him.

Their messages appear on the big screen:

'yes.gr8 2 hear from u. how r u?'
'let's meet 2nite?'
'ok where?'
'rear entrance 2 park nr mcdonalds @ 10pm?'
'ok. c u l8r.'
'bcnu luv dad x'

Mercedes   Look, he says 'luv dad' and a kiss.

Alex   It's a bit of a funny place to meet, isn't it?

Mercedes   Why is it?

Alex   It's a bit spooky round there. I mean, why not the front entrance?

Mercedes   He'll have his reasons. Probably doesn't want anyone to see us, in case he cries.

Alex   Why so late?

Mercedes   I dunno. He's busy, I s'pose.

Alex   It's just a bit odd, that's all.

Mercedes   I'm not spooked. Stop trying to put a damper on things. He's been in touch, that's all that matters.

Alex   Be careful.

Mercedes   Alex, he's my dad; what you trying to say? Here, take this lousy fone back to your dad's and collect your reward.

Alex   What reward? Can I see you tomorrow?

Mercedes   Dunno, I'll have to see what my dad says, won't I?

Scene Twelve

At Dysons' house. **Tetley** *is visiting. They've just finished dinner.*

Tetley   That was a lovely meal, thank you.

Mrs Dyson   My pleasure. I've enjoyed your company.

Tetley   Maybe Alex and Mercedes will join us next time?

Mrs Dyson   She's never in.

Tetley   Alex is the same.

Mrs Dyson   I don't think my daughter really likes me.

Tetley   Nonsense. Alex tells me she never has a bad word to say about you.

Mrs Dyson   That's because she says it all to my face.

Tetley   I think you're a good mother.

Mrs Dyson   Thanks.

Tetley   And a lovely woman.

Mrs Dyson   You're embarrassing me. I'll fetch dessert.

Tetley   Alex and Mercedes seem to have made it up.

Mrs Dyson   I am pleased. She needs a few calming influences does that girl.

There is a knock at the door.

Who can that be at this time? It's nearly ten o'clock.

She goes to the door. It's **Reebok**.

Mrs Dyson   Oh, it's you. What do you want?

Reebok   Can I come in?

Mrs Dyson   No, Reebok, you can't.

Reebok   Can I see Mercedes?

Mrs Dyson   She's not here.

Reebok   Where is she?

Mrs Dyson   Out. I don't know where?

Reebok   Don't you think you should know where she is?

Mrs Dyson   Don't come round here lecturing me how to take care of my daughter.

Reebok   Our daughter.

Mrs Dyson   You wouldn't know it, the way you've behaved.

Reebok   I want to make arrangements to see her, I miss her.

Mrs Dyson   Tough. You wanted it this way, Reebok.

Reebok   Please, can I come in and talk?

Mrs Dyson   Now's not a good time.

Tetley   Is everything all right?

Mrs Dyson   Yes, yes, it's Reebok, Mercedes' dad.

Reebok   Who's that?

Mrs Dyson   None of your business.

Tetley   I'll leave you two alone, if you like. I don't want to intrude on family.

Reebok   Good idea.

Mrs Dyson   No. I'll decide who I have in my house. (*To* **Tetley**.) You stay where you are.

Reebok   I've not come here for an argument. Have you got her mobile number?

Mrs Dyson   Here.

Reebok   Can I borrow your phone?

Mrs Dyson   You cheeky git; you haven't changed, have you?

Reebok   A quick call, see if she's on her way home?

Mrs Dyson   I don't see why I should.

Reebok   Please? I've come all the way, especially.

Mrs Dyson (*handing him the phone*)   Make it quick.

He dials. Elsewhere, **Alex** *appears with* **Mercedes'** *phone, which is ringing.*

Alex   Hello?

Reebok   Who's that?

Alex   Alex.

Reebok   Alex who? (**Tetley** *and* **Mrs Dyson** *are listening.*) Where's Mercedes? Is this her phone?

Alex   Yes, I mean no, I mean it was her fone. Who is this?

Reebok   Is she there?

Alex   No, she's gone to meet her dad – can I ask who's calling?

Reebok   This is her dad – what do you mean she's gone to meet me?

Mrs Dyson   What's going on?

Alex   You text her a message earlier.

Reebok   No, I didn't.

Alex   Yes you did, I was there.

Reebok   It wasn't me.

Alex   Oh, hell.

Reebok   Is this some kind of trick?

Mrs Dyson   Give it here.

She takes the phone off him and hands it to **Tetley**.

Reebok   Oi, what d'you think you're doing?

Mrs Dyson   Alex is his son, let him sort it out.

Tetley (*on the phone*)   Alex?

Alex   Dad? Where are you? What's happening?

Tetley   I'm round at Mrs Dyson's. Where's Mercedes?

Alex   I knew something wasn't right. Dad, you've got to listen to me. Mercedes got a text message from someone pretending to be her dad. She's arranged to meet him at the park near Mcdonald's at ten o'clock.

Tetley   It's ten o'clock now.

Alex   She was meeting him at the back entrance.

Tetley   Leave it to us, Alex. We'll sort it out, don't you go near the park. Wait for me to call.

Tetley *puts down the phone.*

Reebok   I want to know what the hell your son's done with her?

Alex (*on the phone*)   Dad? Dad?

Alex *sighs and runs off.*

Mrs Dyson   Let him speak.

Tetley   There's no time, I'll explain on the way. Get in the car, I'll drive.

Exeunt.

Scene Thirteen

At the park, **Mercedes** *is waiting. It's very spooky. Song 'Wan2tlk'.*

Mercedes   Let me tell you all the things
I wanted you to say,
let me guard your secrets
and convince you you should stay –
when you're a teenage girl,
all alone,
you just wan2tlk.
Let me wish you happiness
and share my dreams with you,
let me ask you questions
and advise me what to do –
when you're growing up fast,
time goes past,
you just wan2tlk.

Love me,
why won't you be my daddy?
Text me, any kind of message,
call me, tell me that you miss me.
Love me,
why won't you be my daddy?
All I want from you:
sing songs to me,
write poetry,
send messages each day.

Let me take you by the hand,
walk with me down the street,
if you came to visit
you would make my life complete –
when you've so much to give,
so much love,
you just wan2tlk.
Let me show you all the things
I've done while you're away,
if you want your daughter

then you only have to say –
when you're a teenage girl,
all alone,
you just wan2tlk.

Love me,
why won't you be my daddy?
Text me, any kind of message,
call me, tell me that you miss me.
Love me,
why won't you be my daddy?
All I want from you:
sing songs to me,
write poetry,
send messages each day.

Mercedes   I wish I had me moby.

There is a noise from the bushes.

Dad? Dad, is that you? Don't be a tease, you know I hate that. I'm coming in.

She passes through a gate and it crashes shut behind her.

Aaargh! (*She realises it's just the gate.*) Scared me to death. Stop messing about. Dad, if that's you, you're frightening me now, it's not fair. I'm warning you, I'll call the police. I've got a moby here the size of a brick, I'll batter you with it.

Alex (*calling*)   I've got them! Mercedes, quick, over here, help me! Aaargh!

Mercedes   Alex!

Alex *staggers out of the darkness, holding his groin and gripping a blanket and rope.*

Mercedes   Alex, you all right? You've been hurt.

Alex   There was two of them. (*He re-creates the incident using her to illustrate events.*) I had my blanket over them like this, I was trying to tie them up –

Reebok *rushes on and tackles* **Alex** *to the floor.*

Reebok   I've got him! I've got him!

Alex   Aargh! Let me go! It wasn't me, I swear!

Mercedes (*pulling* **Reebok** *off* **Alex**)   Dad, Dad, put him down, that's Alex.

Reebok   I don't care who it is, I'm having him.

Mercedes (*breaking* **Alex** *free*)   It wasn't him, let him go.

Tetley *and* **Mrs Dyson** *appear.* **Alex** *runs to* **Tetley**. **Mrs Dyson** *comforts* **Mercedes**.

Mrs Dyson   Thank god you're all right.

Mercedes   Thank Alex, he saved me.

Reebok   I tried to save you.

Mercedes   I don't understand. What about your messages?

Alex   You were set up, Mercedes. Somebody's trying to frighten you.

Mercedes   What have I done to deserve this?

Mrs Dyson   Let's get you home, we can call the police from there.

Mercedes   No police!

Mrs Dyson   Okay, okay.

Reebok   We don't need police, if I get a hold of them.

Mrs Dyson   That's all we need.

Reebok   I'm not having anybody frightening my little girl. I'll show 'em scary.

Mercedes   Did you really come to see me, Dad?

Reebok   I did. I want us to see each other regular.

Mercedes   I'd like that, if Mum agrees.

Mrs Dyson   I was never the one standing in the way.

Alex (*to* **Mercedes**)   Meet me tomorrow before school, I think I know who it is.

Exeunt.

Scene Fourteen

Outside school the next day. **Alex** *and* **Mercedes** *are in hiding, listening to* **Gucchi**, **Nike** *and the others.*

Nike   You should have seen her: she was petrified.

Gucchi   It was well funny.

Cream   Did she not suspect it was a wind-up?

Gucchi   Did she heck? She fell for it straight away.

Nike   You know what she's like: 'Daddy buys me this, Daddy buys me that' – she makes me sick.

Gucchi   She's a little thief, her old man doesn't buy her anything.

Nike   'My daddy's always sending me messages cos my daddy loves me.'

Beemer   Her dad's a right pervert hanging round the park like that.

Gucchi   It wasn't really her dad, thicko, it was us.

Chelsea   What happened in the end?

Gucchi   Dunno, we had to leg it.

Nike   Some perve threw his jacket on us, trying to tie us up, can you believe it?

Diesel   You get some right nutters in that park, don't you?

Beemer   I don't get it? I thought you said her dad wasn't really there?

Gucchi   Somebody explain to him in words of less than two syllables.

Cream   Weren't you frightened?

Gucchi   No way. I kicked him in the nads. I shouldn't think he'll be feeling very pervy for a while.

Diesel   You should have battered him.

Gucchi   We'd blown it by then, we had to get away.

Exeunt.

Alex   Did you hear that? They didn't realise it was me.

Mercedes   They think they're so hard.

Alex   I've seen the messages they send to each other, Gucchi and Nike, they're well soppy; it's embarrassing.

Mercedes   They're so two-faced, somebody should expose them for who they really are.

Alex   I'm glad you said that. I've got a plan.

Mercedes   Tell me more.

Alex   It's PE this morning in the hall. While they're doing gym, we'll nip into the lockers and rob their mobies. I know how to connect the fones to the PC that's connected to the digital projector in the hall.

Mercedes   To do what?

Alex   Don't you get it? While everyone's in the hall, we'll project all their text messages and show everyone what they're really like.

Mercedes   That would be so sweet. I'll rob Nike's, you rob Gucchi's.

Alex   I'll meet you in the projector room.

Scene Fifteen

School hall which doubles as a gym. **Gucchi**, **Beemer** *and* **Diesel** *are larking about, playing basketball with* **Nike**, **Cream** *and* **Chelsea**. *Other classmates are hanging about in the gym. As messages start scrolling on the big screen, a computer-generated voice reads the messages through loudspeakers. The messages start with* **Gucchi** *and* **Nike** *slagging their mates* **Beemer**, **Diesel**, **Cream** *and* **Chelsea**. **Gucchi** *and* **Nike** *try to protest about what's happening but the damage is done.* **Beemer**, **Diesel**, **Cream** *and* **Chelsea** *fall out with them and move away to the other side of the hall.* **Gucchi** *and* **Nike** *are isolated, forced to listen to a series of embarrassingly soppy messages to each other. As a result, they fall out with each other and storm off as everyone laughs at them.*

Scene Sixteen

Outside Dysons' house. **Mercedes** *and* **Alex** *are met by* **Reebok**. **Alex** *retires, to leave them alone to talk.*

Reebok   Your mam told me what happened with the shoplifting and that.

Mercedes   Don't you start, I'm ashamed enough as it is.

Reebok   No, I feel ashamed, I should have been there for you. I've bought you a present. (*He hands it to her.*)

Mercedes   Thanks. It's a new moby.

Reebok   Alex told me which one you'd like.

Mercedes   I don't know what to say.

Reebok   Don't say anything, just send me a text message.

Mercedes   I will. I'll send you loads.

Reebok   I won't lose touch again, I promise. Come and visit me, you're welcome any time.

Mercedes   I will.

Reebok   And bring Alex.

Mercedes   I'd like that.

Reebok (*leaving*)   Later.

Mercedes   Later, Dad.

She texts a message immediately which appears on the big screen:

'luv u dad. M xx'
'luv u daughter. bye. bcnu. dad xx'

Scene Seventeen

*Enter **Jade**. **Mercedes** and **Alex** appear on the big screen, looking in at her in her cyber-arcade.*

Jade   You people make me laugh,
you find it so hard to communicate,
you've got gadgets galore,
yet you can't talk straight.
Radios and TVs,
computers and DVDS,
telephones and mobile phones,
a million ways to be alone.
You'd think 'I love you' was a virus
it's so hard for you to say it –
how can three little words
seem so toxic?
Thousands of words in your vocabulary
and yet you rely on grunts like
'urgh, er, argh, mmm, innit,
okay, yeah, no,
hiya, seeya, you see,
right, you know'.
Open your mouth,
wiggle your tongue
and before very long
you won't be able to stop the words.

You run around like mad-arse flies
as if you're always late
for an important appointment,
you don't know how to communicate.
Just stop for a minute:
try saying 'hello' to a complete stranger,
instead of getting on his case,
or talk to the person next to you
and put a smile on both your faces,
spare a few words as well as pennies
for the beggar on the street,
you'd be surprised how many people you meet
want to tell you their stories.
Take it from me, the Diva of Cool,
one simple rule:
on the catwalk of life,
you need the style of a leopard
and the eyes of a hawk;
but most of all you need to talk the talk.
If you wan2tlk,
just do it,
It's cool to talk.

End with full cast in a final blast of 'Allerton Boys, Allerton Girls'.

Stuff I Buried in a Small Town

Mike Bartlett

About the Author

Mike Bartlett was born in Abingdon, Oxfordshire and currently lives in London. His plays include *Contractions* (Royal Court), *My Child* (Royal Court), *Artefacts* (Nabokov/Bush Theatre). Adaptations include *The Lesson* (Arcola). Radio includes *Love Contract* (Radio 4), *The Family Man* (Radio 4) and *Not Talking* (Radio 3).

Mike Barlett was Pearsons Playwright in Residence at the Royal Court Theatre in 2007. He won the Writers Guild Tinniswood and Imison prizes for *Not Talking*, and the Old Vic New Voices Award for *Artefacts*.

About the Play

The play was commissioned by the Hampstead Theatre for their 16–18 Heat and Light Company. They were after a play which set them challenges in terms of form and content and which had substantial parts for all twenty in the group. I wanted to write a play about a town away from London, much like the one I grew up in.

The original production in spring 2006 at Hampstead Theatre's Michael Frayn Studio was directed by Kelly Wilkinson for the Heat and Light Company. The design was by Nathalie Frost, lighting by Mark Jones, and sound by Dean Puzey and Dominic Butcher. I was amazed by the energy, commitment and passion during rehearsals. At one point we had about eight different scenes being practised at any one time. The actors were phenomenal, carefully discovering their characters' intentions, and then playing it in performance as though it was the most important thing in the world. A writer can't ask for more than that.

Drama is all about people doing things to each other. In every single line of this play someone is doing something to someone else. When you act it, see what happens when you go at speed and really earn the pauses that are written. With any luck the scene will become electric – suddenly work like football, and the audience will sit forward and react accordingly, watching and listening carefully, unsure as to who might 'foul', who might get 'sent off' and who might, finally, score.

This play is about when we're active and when we're passive. It is not a city play. It is very much about a small town. As the Sociologist says, these towns have their own rules and the important thing is that the audience understands, that this town is, for these people, the whole world.

A word about scene changes: if at all possible, avoid them, don't even pause, just go straight on with the play. Set the scene with performance and attitude, and the script will help. Theatre like this is about the people, what they do and why they do it.

Make it your own, make it something to remember and most importantly, no matter what, be sure you enjoy it.

Characters

Danny, *seventeen / twenty-three, white*
Craig, *seventeen, white*
Stuart, *twenty-two*
Krissie, *eighteen, black*
Gary, *eighteen*
Raf, *sixteen, white*
Tyler, *seventeen, white*
Paul, *eighteen, white*
Harriet, *twenty-two*
Tom, *twenty-three*
Natalie, *sixteen*
Emma, *fourteen*
Hayley, *sixteen*
Carly, *fifteen*
Zara, *sixteen*
Darren, *twenty*
Bryony, *eighteen*
Ed, *nineteen*
Jo, *nineteen*
Suze, *eighteen*
Nurse, *twenty-two*
James, *twenty-two*
Anthea, *twenty-two*
The Sociologist, *twenty-three / twenty-seven*

(/) means the next speech begins at that point.
(–) means the next line interrupts.
*(. . .) at the end of a speech means it trails off. On its own, it indicates
a pressure, expectation or desire to speak.*
*A speech with no written dialogue indicates a character deliberately
remaining silent.*
Blank space between speeches in the dialogue indicates time drifting on.

*The play must move very quickly and fluidly. Characters and scenes can
arise anywhere, overlap, confuse and occur without warning. The
playing should be brutal and passionate, surprising and dangerous. It
must feel on the point of collapsing, but never actually do so.*

Scene One

Sociologist   Alright. Settle down.

Can I begin?

Right. Can I remind you of the new directive agreed by the department that if a mobile phone rings in a lecture the lecture will be automatically and immediately terminated. I intend to follow that procedure. Alright?

So.

A small southern British town can be extremely isolated. The town may once have had a brewery, a port, a car factory or an airbase, but for…

She looks at someone in the lecture hall not paying attention. Waits for it.

For . . . different reasons these industries have now moved or closed down, the workforce commutes somewhere else, and although a minority of people may still attempt to hold the community together through religious, sporting or cultural activities, most adults see the town as simply the place where their house happens to stand.

Craig   Stuart!

Sociologist   But for the young people, this town is their world, for them its edges are like high walls,

Craig   My brother's mate, remember? / I told you.

Sociologist   The town has its own rules, / its own struggles and divisions.

Stuart   What's your name?

Sociologist   . . . they can feel like they will never leave, and for some of them, that will prove to be true.

The landfill. First thing in the morning.

Danny   Danny.

Stuart   How old are you?

Danny   Sixteen.

Stuart   School?

Danny   No.

Stuart   What?

Danny   Left.

Stuart   When?

Danny   Couple of months?

Stuart   What have you done since you left school?

Danny   Tried to get a job. Got one. Hated it. Nothing.

Stuart   What job?

Danny   Spar.

Stuart   What happened?

Danny   I hit my boss round the face with a tin…

Stuart   A tin?

Danny   Of soup. And we thought it best I leave after that.

Stuart   Why?

Danny   He said he couldn't trust me.

Stuart   Why did you hit him?

Danny   He said I was stupid.

Stuart   Listen. I'm gonna do you a favour. You're a mate of Craig's, and –

Danny   I know his brother.

Stuart   Craig says you'll work hard.

Danny   I will.

Stuart   Good.

Danny   I will work hard.

Stuart   Do you know what you'll be doing?

Danny   Trucks is it?

Stuart   Not quite. I'm going to give you this. It's called a fork. You pick up stray bits of rubbish round the site.

Danny   I thought I would drive the trucks.

Craig does.

Stuart   You're not old enough.

And Craig's done a course.

Danny   Shit man.

Stuart   Danny. At least you're not answering phones for the carphone craphouse, you'll be out on a landfill, getting fit, doing something mankind is good at: burying its shit.

Best job in the world.

You get used to the smell.

So do you still want it or shall I call the agency?

Danny   Yeah.

Stuart   Right. You'll be in a team with this lot. This is Paul, Tyler and – what's your name?

Raf   Raf.

Stuart   Raf. Are you new?

Raf   No.

Stuart   Oh.

Raf   Jesus.

Stuart   Danny, come by the office at the end of the day to do your form.

Danny   I appreciate you giving me this chance to prove myself.

Stuart   Good.

Danny   I promise I'll work hard.

Stuart   If you get on alright here, you'll be driving the trucks in no time.

Emma   Natalie.

Paul (*singing to Danny*)   Eenee meenee mynee mo
Catch a nigger / by his toe.

Emma   Natalie!

Paul   If he hollers fuck his shit.
You're going closest to the edge of the pit. Ha.

Emma   Natalie?

Natalie?

Natalie'*s front room. She's watching television.*

Natalie   What?

Emma   You going out tonight?

Natalie   Yeah.

Emma   You meeting a boy? Cos Sarah at school told me you're meeting Danny Butler for a date.

Natalie?

Natalie   WHAT?

Emma   Are ya?

Natalie   YEAH!

Emma   ALRIGHT!

Natalie?

Have you done it yet?

With a boy?

Natalie   What? *Done it* done it?

Emma   Nah not done it done it.

Natalie   What then?

Emma   Got off.

Natalie   Course.

Emma   Oh.

Natalie?

Natalie   . . .

Emma   You know when you kiss then?

Natalie   Yeah.

Emma   Do you put your tongue in?

Natalie   Yeah.

Emma   I didn't.

Is he gonna think I'm weird?

Natalie   No.

Emma   Did you bump your teeth?

Natalie   What?

Emma   Did you bump your teeth?

Natalie   No.

Emma   We did. I must have been crap.

Natalie   Shut up. I'm sure you were . . . alright.

Emma   Alright? God. Isn't fourteen a bit late to get off with someone? How old were you?

Natalie   Don't know. Probably couple of years ago, Fourteen. Yeah.

Emma   Where?

Natalie   On holiday. Majorca.

Emma   I didn't see you.

Natalie   Yeah, well . . . It was with this guy on the beach, you went to get an ice cream. You was a kid. You wouldn't . . .

Emma   You going to kiss Daniel Butler tonight though?

Natalie   No.

I don't know.

Krissie   This reading . . .

Natalie   Maybe.

Krissie *is standing by Lilly's recently filled grave, reading from a Bible.*

Krissie   . . . is Lilly's favourite and is taken from the Book of Luke, chapter six, verses twenty-seven to thirty-one.

'But I tell you who hear me: Love your enemies, do good to those who hate you. If someone strikes you on one cheek, turn to him the other also.

Harriet *is in her flat and anxious.*
She pours herself a glass of wine and sips it.

Harriet *gets two boxes. One large, one small. They are both from Tesco.*

Krissie   Do to others as you would have them do to you.'

Harriet *opens the large box. It is a birthday cake.*
She opens the small one. Candles.

She places a few candles on the cake.

She goes back to her glass of wine.
Checks her watch.

Worried.

Lights the candles.

Tom *enters wearing a suit, and holding a briefcase.*

Harriet *smiles at him, lights the candles and sings 'Happy*
Birthday' to **Tom**.

Tom *cries*

Harriet   I was hoping you might smile.

Tom   Well I was hoping I might look at you and find you
attractive again, but sometimes we don't get the things we
want do we?

Dog.

Do we?

Ed   She always loved hearing it read out.

Krissie, **Gary**, **Ed**, **Jo**, **Suze**, **Bryony** *and* **Darren** *are*
standing around a new grave.
Harriet *blows out the candles.*

Gary   Why couldn't you go to the actual thing?

Bryony   It was family only.

Ed   They didn't want any of the groups there.

Suze   Not even her favourite group.

Gary   Who was her favourite group?

The whole group look up at **Gary**.

Oh.

She was good, then?

Darren   She was wonderful.

Suze   Isn't it weird? We're all only seven feet away from her right now?

Ed   Yeah.

Jo   That's just her body.

Suze   Yeah. Down there. Her face. Hands. Fingernails. All turning to dust.

Ed   I'm going for cremation. Burn me up to heaven. I don't want to rot.

Krissie   Do you all really believe in that?

Ed   What?

Krissie   Heaven?

Ed   Yeah.

Darren   Yes.

Bryony   Don't you?

Krissie   I can't believe Lilly's watching us now. I can't feel her.

It's just nothing. She's gone.

Jo   She wouldn't want you saying that.

Krissie   I want to –

Jo   You mustn't let death shake you. This life is only the beginning.

Krissie   I try to keep thinking that's true but –

Jo   You believe in God though?

Krissie   . . .

Jo   The Holy Spirit.

Jesus?

Krissie   Yes.

Jo   But not heaven? Not an eternal soul?

Krissie   I don't know.

Jo   Lilly wouldn't want you to say that.

Darren   Jo –

Jo   She wouldn't.

Suze   Jo.

Jo   What?

Suze   She wouldn't get angry.

Jo   Can we just do this please? I'm cold.

Bryony   Yeah come on.

They all pick up a handful of dirt. **Krissie** *prompts* **Gary** *to do the same.*

Darren   Shall I go first?

Lilly. Thank you for helping me to feel more comfortable in my own skin.

He throws his dirt on to the grave.

Suze   You were the grandmother I never had.

She throws her dirt on to the grave.
Bryony *has her eyes closed.*

Bryony   French bread. Eyelashes. Damascus.

She throws the earth down.

Ed   Lilly, I threw up on you when I was seven, and unlike many girls since you never held that against me. Thank you.

He throws the dirt down. **Gary** *is next in line.*

Gary   Er . . . Lilly. You're dead now and I never met you so I don't know what you were like. But you sounded great so . . . yeah. Well done.

He throws his dirt down.

Jo   Lilly, let Jesus's love embrace you now for ever.

Stay with me, and I'll see you soon.

Jo *throws the earth down.*

Krissie   Lilly . . . I . . .

Sorry.

She's just gone hasn't she?

She can't hear us.

Krissie *turns away and brushes her hands of dirt.*

Paul   I thought you was gonna be a black boy.

Krissie *slowly walks off.* **Darren** *looks at* **Gary**.
Gary *follows her.*

The landfill. Tea break.

Danny   What?

Tyler   Him?

Paul   Yeah.

Tyler   He isn't.

Paul   I know. But I thought he was gonna be.

Tyler   Why?

Paul   Way Craig spoke before. Like he was ashamed of
him.

Raf   Probably cos he's quiet. Aren't you? Hello?

Paul   If you had've been a brother you know what I'd
have done?

Raf *and* **Tyler** *laugh.* **Danny** *smiles.*

Danny   No.

Paul   It's not funny.

If you was a brother it would be no laughing matter.

Danny   What?

Paul *goes over to* **Danny** *and aggressively acts it out.*

Paul   If you was a brother, I'd do what I did last time. I'd
get this bright white sheet and one day after work, when you
was getting changed in the cabin, I'd put it on and creep up
to the door. Then I'd burst in on you, wearing it on my face
with holes cut out yeah? Cut out for the mouth and eyes,
you know like the Ku Klux Klan. Like a ghost. You'd shit
yourself.

It would run down your legs.

Danny   You done this?

Paul   Yeah. Then I pushed him against the wall and said I
was going to string him up like a goat.

Tyler*'s laughing.*

Tyler   So wrong.

Paul   His face!

Tyler *does an impression.*

Tyler   What the! What the . . . Shit! Help! Oooo.

Paul   Hey.

Stuart *walks in. The atmosphere changes. They are now quiet and keep their heads down.*

Stuart   Alright boys.

They all mumble a reply.

Hello Danny.

Danny   Alright.

Stuart   Getting on okay?

Danny   Yeah. Thanks.

Stuart   They looking after you?

Danny   Yes.

Stuart   Good good.

Stuart *would like to have a conversation, but no one will.*

Right.

Good. See you boys later then.

He walks off.

Paul   See you boys later. Twat.

Danny   Why do you hate them so much?

Paul   What?

Danny   I can't be bothered with them, but I don't wanna kill them.

Paul   I do. Fucking gas 'em.

Raf *laughs.*

Raf   Jesus.

Tyler   Why not?

Paul   That would shut them up.

Raf   You're a mentalist, mate.

Paul   Yeah.

Raf   But I love ya.

Paul   Shut up. Gay.

Craig *enters*.

Paul   You're coming out tonight aren't you Craig?

Craig   Tonight?

Paul   Yeah. Down the Grapes?

Craig   Yeah.

(*To Danny*.) You coming?

Danny   No.

Craig   Why not?

Danny   I'm meeting Natalie.

Craig   Meating –

Danny   We're going out.

Craig   Where?

Danny   Pizza Express.

They laugh.

What? Craig mate, I need you to come too.

Craig   What? No. Why?

Danny   She thinks it's a few of us meeting up.

Craig   Why does she think that?

Danny   That's what I told her.

So she'd say yes.

The boys all laugh.

Craig   You twat. Fuck it. Come with us.

Danny   No.

I like her.

Craig   You like her.

Craig *takes something out of his bag. It's covered.*
He hides it from **Danny***, but shows it to* **Paul***.*

You have to come out tonight Daniel, because you work
here now and we're having a work night out.

Danny   I can't.

Craig   No?

Paul *and* **Craig** *both laugh.*
Tyler *and* **Raf** *go and have a look.*
They laugh.

Natalie *is getting ready to go out. Doing her make-up. Her hair is
curled and she is choosing a top. She looks almost on the point of
crying. The phone starts vibrating on the table.* **Natalie** *gets out the
hands-free. Plugs it in.*

Danny   What is it?

Craig *shows* **Danny***. It's a knife.*

Craig   You'll want it tonight.

Danny   No.

Paul   Don't be a pussy.

Danny   I'm not.

Natalie *answers the phone.*

Natalie   Yeah. / Alright Hayley.

Paul   I'll tell Stuart you're a pussy.

Danny   I'm . . .

Paul   No trucks for you / mate.

Hayley   Alright girl. How's you?

Natalie   Yeah. Good.

Natalie *stops doing her lipstick halfway. Her hand drops. She just looks at herself in the mirror.*

The boys look at **Danny***. He takes the knife. They laugh.* **Raf** *slaps him on the arm affectionately.*

Natalie *looks at herself from the side in the mirror, pushes her chin around. She's not happy with what she sees. She puts the make-up down and pushes her chair away from the table.*

Hayley   I finished it with Simon.

Natalie *stands up aimlessly. Feels awful. Looks down at herself. Her clothes. She looks at herself in the mirror.*

Hayley   He bought me this ring, but then when I was wearing it at school, Carly says she recognises it yeah?

Natalie *looks at herself sideways.*

Hayley   And she was sure she'd seen Nicky Reynolds with it about four months ago. So I asked Simon yeah and he said no he'd bought it for me, but I knew that he had that thing with Nicky Reynolds so I asks him again yeah?

Natalie *despairs, undoes her hair and ruffs it around.*

Hayley   And I say he better tell the truth this time yeah . . . or you know . . . you know? So then he says he did buy it for her originally but when they split up she gave it him back, and he didn't . . . get this . . . didn't want to waste it. So I just shouted at him in Woolworth's. Just shouted his name. Siimon! Siiiimon! I was so pissed off. I grabbed this pick 'n' mix and threw it in his face. Then they made *him* pay for it. He's now banned from Woolworth's! But yeah, so I'm well up for it tonight. Are you ready for your dinner party?

Natalie *pinches her waist to see how much fat there is.*

Hayley   You looking sexy? You gonna pull him? He's shy but he so wants you. When was the last time you got off with someone?

When was it?

Natalie *sits in the chair and stares at the ground.*

Hayley   You wearing something nice, yeah?

Natalie   Yeah.

She screws up the top and throws it in a corner. Twirls her hair with her finger nervously.

Hayley   Wicked. Oh yeah, don't curl your hair. You looks better with it straight, yeah? Have a good time. See ya.

Natalie   Bye.

She hangs up.

Scene Two

Krissie and **Gary** *are in Pizza Express.*

Krissie   I can't believe I did that.

I just couldn't talk to her like that and mean it, you know? And if I mean it then what's the point?

Do you think they were annoyed?

I know you don't like them, but they're good people.

It meant so much to me that you came along.

Did they piss you off?

Is that the problem?

Gary   No.

Krissie   But there is . . . a problem?

Gary.

Since we sat down I've been terrified that this is a break-up dinner. That at any point you're going to start a sentence with 'Look Krissie, I just think . . .' and before you get any further, I'll know that we're over.

Tell me that's not what this is.

Gary I . . .

Krissie   Tell me that's not what this is.

Oh. It is. That's it. That was it. Wasn't it?

Oh.

Why?

I want to make it work.

Gary I don't think . . .

Krissie   Why do this to me here? In public?

Gary I thought it would be nice.

Krissie   What?

Nice?

Pizza Express?

What's wrong with me?

Gary Nothing.

Krissie   . . .

Gary It isn't the same as it used to be.

Krissie   We're only on the starters.

Gary We've been going out nearly a year.

Krissie   No. We're only on the starters. The dough balls. We're having a whole meal. And you tell me we're over now?

Gary   We can leave if you want.

Krissie   No, you don't just do this. I'm going to talk you round.

We're going to have these starters, then mains, then dessert, then coffee, and then we're going to go on to the Grapes for drinks. I've got ages.

I'm going to make this a very long evening.

Natalie *enters.*

Natalie   Hi. / Sorry I'm late.

Danny   That's alright.

Natalie   Where's everyone else?

Danny   They couldn't come.

Natalie   Oh.

Why not?

Danny   They went out instead. I tried to call you but . . .

Natalie   That's annoying.

Danny   Yeah.

Natalie   Yeah. So. What, you want to . . . ? I mean . . . we could do something.

If you want.

Danny   Do you?

Natalie   Not bothered.

Danny   I'm not bothered either.

Natalie   Unless there's something you really want to do.

Danny   Like what?

Natalie   Don't know.

Cinema or something?

Danny   What film?

Natalie   Don't know.

New Harry Potter I suppose.

Danny   You like Harry Potter?

Natalie   No . . . well . . . you know . . . it's on. Do you?

Danny   It's alright. So, do you want to see that then?

Natalie   Not if you don't.

Danny   I don't mind.

Natalie   Shall I sit down then?

Danny   Up to you.

Natalie   Well are we doing something or not?

Danny   You don't really seem up for it.

Natalie   So shall we just . . .

Danny   What?

Natalie   What?

Danny   Shall we just . . . what? Go . . .

Natalie   Go . . . somewhere?

Danny   You mean meet up with the others?

Natalie   If you want.

Danny   Okay.

Natalie   Okay then.

Danny   Alright. Wait a minute

Danny *downs the rest of the pint, picks up his coat and leaves.*
Natalie *stands for a moment. Then follows.*

Natalie   Okay.

The Grapes.

Hayley   They've got this new cocktail at the bar. It's called a shag.

Zara   A what?

Hayley   A shag.

So I said to the barman – he's fit yeah – I said I wanted three shags.

They laugh.

Carly   Only three?

Hayley   Piss off. No. Then he said alright darling, and what is it to drink?

She laughs.

Carly   You're in there Hayley.

Hayley   Nah. Parently he's a twat actually.

Zara   Is that Natalie?

Carly   Yeah.

Zara   Who's she with?

Hayley   That Danny.

Carly   Oi!

Natalie   Alright?

Hayley   Mental!

Zara   Hiya.

Carly   Hi.

Natalie This is Danny. We thought we'd come and find you. His mates are out too.

Hayley Right.

Danny Hi.

Hayley Alright. What do you do Danny?

Danny Just started on the landfill.

Zara Doesn't that smell of shit?

Danny No. I drive the trucks.

Natalie Do you?

Danny Yeah.

Carly Okay.

Hayley Natalie, I'm having a shag. Do you want one?

Natalie What? I've just got here.

Hayley It's a cocktail at the bar. A shag.

Natalie Oh.

Hayley Do you want one?

Danny I'll get it.

Hayley Oh. Alright.

Natalie Okay.

Out of the club suddenly appear **Craig**, **Tyler**, **Paul** *and* **Raf**. *They grab* **Danny** *and chant at him loudly.*

Craig Danny boy. Danniiii Boyyy!

Paul Alright, gayer.

Tyler Is this homosexual bothering you girls?

Hayley No.

Raf Doesn't look like he'd bother much does he?

I'm Raf.

Carly   Alright boys.

Natalie   Are these your mates?

Danny   Yeah.

Zara   Hello.

Paul   Which of you young ladies wants a shag?

Craig   What you doing here? / I thought you was on a date. With that girl. What was her name?

Hayley   I'll have another / one if you're offering.

Danny   Natalie.

Zara   Yeah alright.

Craig   What happened?

Paul   Tyler. Buy the ladies a drink.

Tyler   Ohhhh. Alright. Two shags.

Carly   And me.

Tyler   Three shags.

Natalie   Danny's getting me one.

Craig   Are you Natalie?

Natalie   Yeah.

Craig   Shit.

Yeah. You let Danny get you a shag.

What's going on?

Danny   Nothing. Leave it.

Craig   Nothing?

Right.

Well maybe you needs a few drinks now then yeah?

Danny   Yeah.

Craig   Go to the bar. Dry your eyes. Drown your sorrows in a triple aftershock.

Tyler   Come on.

Danny   Alright.

They go.

Natalie   How do you know Danny?

Craig   Friend of his brother's. We work on the landfill. I drive the trucks.

Natalie   Like Danny.

Craig   What?

Natalie   Danny. He drive the trucks.

Craig   Nah. He only started today. Is that what he told you? No. He picks up shit off the floor with a fork.

Natalie   Oh.

Craig *turns to* **Zara**.

Craig   Right girl, come and get it with me dancing.

Zara   Is that your best line?

Craig   Always works.

Zara   Come on. Girls, you coming?

Natalie   I'm gonna stay here.

Hayley   Me too.

Zara   Carly?

Carly   Be there in a minute.

Zara   Come on then boys.

Zara *goes off with* **Paul**, **Tyler** *and* **Raf**.

Hayley   You alright Natalieeee!?

Natalie   Is this top alright?

Hayley   What? Yeah. It is. Sexy.

Carly   Yeah.

Natalie   Okay.

Carly   Why?

Natalie   No. I just thought it made me look fat.

Carly   It doesn't make you look fat.

Hayley   No.

Natalie   Would you actually tell me if it did though?

Hayley   Yeah. Probably. Probably.

Natalie   Nah. You wouldn't. Cos you'd think it would upset me.

Carly   It would upset you though wouldn't it, if we was to tell you you was fat.

Natalie   Yeah.

Carly   Well then.

They all go back to their drinks except **Natalie**.

Natalie   So what're you saying?

Carly   Alright, look. Honestly Natalie what I think is that that top is not the best top you've ever worn but you look alright and if you get pissed it won't matter.

Natalie   Right.

Hayley   Nice one Carly.

Carly   What? She wanted to know.

Natalie   Yeah I did.

I did.

Hayley   Let's go dance.

Natalie   I'll stay here?

Carly   Alright.

Hayley   Come over in a minute. Bring Danny.

Natalie   Alright.

They get up and go. **Natalie** *is left by herself.*
Danny *comes over with a drink.*

Natalie   Thanks.

Why d'you tell me you drove the trucks?

Danny   I do.

Natalie   Your mate said you pick up shit off the floor.

Danny   I'm gonna drive the trucks. Soon.

I am.

Harriet *stands facing* **Tom**, *exactly as the end of their last scene.*

Tom   Why did you blow my candles out?

Harriet   You were crying.

Tom   I hate the sound of your voice.

Harriet   What's the matter?

Tom   It's not a happy birthday is it?

Harriet   I thought it could be.

Tom   I have to go to work, where no one cares about me, on my birthday. I get pulled into a meeting, with everyone, and get accused of not pulling my weight. And then I get home, and you blow out my candles.

On my birthday.

He looks at her, desperate.

Even today you hate me so why don't you leave? I wish you would.

Harriet *sits down next to him.*

She puts a hand on his shoulder, which he pushes off immediately and violently.

Harriet   Make a wish, Tom.

Tom   I've run out of pills.

Harriet   Why didn't you say?

That's why you feel like this.

Tom   It's nothing to do with that.

Harriet   Okay.

Tom   It's you.

You and your voice. Tell me that you've done something wrong today. You've got it wrong and upset me. Again. Haven't you?

Harriet   I love you.

Tom   Answer my question.

Harriet   I love you.

Tom   Answer my question dog.

Harriet   . . .

Tom   So I'm just being mental?

Harriet   I think we should get the pills.

Tom   Fuck off.

Harriet *puts on her coat.*

Tom   I don't want them.

Harriet   I'm not getting the pills.

Tom   Where you going then?

Harriet   I'm leaving.

Harriet *packs a small bag.*

Tom   I'm ill.

Harriet   And I'm a very loving girlfriend and a good person but you're bringing me down with you and I can't go there any more. I'm making this worse.

I'm sorry I'm not stronger.

Tom   You don't care about me.

It's late. Where you going to go?

Harriet   I don't know. Eat the cake.

Harriet *leaves.*

Hayley   Taxi!

Zara   Hayley.

Hayley   Taxi!

Zara   There's a queue. Ooo. Ooo. There's a bit of a queue!

Hayley   Leave this to me.

Carly   Can I not stand now please?

Zara   You've got to.

Carly   No.

Carly *collapses to the floor.*

Better.

Zara   Oh shit. Hayley. Come here. Natalie. Give me a hand.

Natalie *goes over and they support* **Carly** *between them.*

Carly   Piss off. The floor's cold. I want to . . . I want to . . . Hey! Boys! Hello boys!

The boys come out of the club.
Tyler *goes straight up to* **Carly** *and starts to kiss her.*

Craig   Alright girls. Had a good time?

Hayley   Yeah.

Danny   Alright.

Natalie   Hi.

Zara   We're getting a taxi, wanna share?

Craig   No. We're all going back to my place. Saxon Road. You should come.

Hayley   Sorry boys. It's our bedtime. Natalie you could go.

Natalie   It's okay.

Paul   Danny. Did you get off with her?

Danny   What? No.

Paul   Why not?

Danny   . . .

Paul   Do it now.

Danny   No.

Raf   Yeah. Why not? Do her.

Do her! Do her! Do her!

The Boys   Do her! Do her! Do her!

Craig   Come on Danny. What are you? Gay. Do you not fancy her?

Danny   Nah.

Look at her. Too porky in't she?

Paul *bursts out laughing.*

Hayley   Oi! Twat.

Paul   Shut up, he's just saying it like it is.

Hayley   Come on Natalie. Let's go.

Natalie   Yeah.

Zara   Oi. Carly. Come on.

Carly *looks up, confused, waves to* **Tyler** *and follows them.*

Danny   Natalie.

Natalie *goes.*

Paul   Don't matter. Come on.

Danny   Shit!

Krissie *appears. She is a bit drunk and walking ahead of* **Gary**, *who is following. They both look very unhappy.*

Danny *is angry and bangs into* **Krissie** *accidentally. She pushes him out of the way.*

Paul   Oi, bitch, got a light?

Krissie   Go away.

Paul   What?

Krissie   Piss off.

Paul   What?

She pushes past him.

Watch your mouth.

Paul *pushes* **Krissie**.

Harriet *appears, and watches at a distance.*

Gary *has caught up.*

Gary   Come on Krissie.

Paul   Black nigger nigger bitch.

Krissie   Fuck / you.

Paul   Wog.

Paki.

Coon.

Tyler and **Raf** *hit* **Gary** *on the back of the head.*

Gary   Krissie!

Gary *runs away, but* **Paul** *trips* **Krissie** *and she falls on to the ground.* **Harriet** *calls the police.*

Paul   Danny.

Danny   What?

Paul   The knife.

Danny   No.

Paul   Cut.

Cut her.

Danny *cuts* **Krissie** *across the face, she screams.*

Craig   Let's fuck off.

The boys run away.

Krissie *lying on the ground crying. Unconscious and bleeding.* **Gary** *is standing at a distance.*

Harriet *comes forward and gets a tissue out of her bag to stop the bleeding.*

Gary   Is she alright?

Harriet   Are you her boyfriend?

Gary   No.

Harriet   What's her name?

Gary   Krissie.

Harriet   Are you her boyfriend?

Why didn't you do anything?

Sirens. Blue flashing light. **Gary** *runs off.*

Krissie.

Krissie?

Darren *stands at his door.*

Gary *is outside, cold, upset.*

They look at each other.

They hug.

Darren   What happened?

Was she upset?

Did you tell her?

Gary   She's been attacked. Cut with a knife. I didn't do anything.

Darren   Is she alright?

Gary   I didn't stop them, and then she was on the ground and there was this other girl. She asked why I didn't help. I ran away and . . .

I can't go back now.

Darren   We could go to the hospital.

Gary   Maybe I shouldn't be here either.

Darren   Do you want to come in?

It's alright.

Gary   Yes please.

Darren *puts his arms around him.*

Gary   I'm sorry. I'm sorry.

Darren   It's alright.

Danny *stands on the edge of the landfill at night with a shovel.*

He takes the knife out.

He throws it down into the ground.

He gets the shovel.

Craig *appears behind him.*

Craig   Alright?

Danny   Yeah. I'm alright.

Craig   You okay?

Danny   Shit.

Shit.

Craig   Just bury it.

Danny   Yeah. Yeah.

Yeah.

Craig   Forget it.

Danny   Yeah.

Danny *buries the knife with rubbish.*

Craig *wanders off.*

Danny *stands, looking at the floor.*

Scene Three

Sociologist   Of course we know that the violence and
alienation in a small town arises from the enclosed
community, dividing itself into groups and treating the town

as their territory. Race, religion, housing estate, money or sexuality can all be lines down which the town is divided. In our present cultural moment, these prejudices are likely to remain under the surface, and only occasionally bubble up. If they do, however, it only takes a spark for the situation to ignite, and create a blaze.

The landfill. The boys are sitting around eating sandwiches.

Tyler   It's blood. The way I see it racism is entirely natural. We're all animals, and we're all tribal. It's normal to want to protect your own. We are a different race from them. We're white and they are genetically different. Yeah, they look different but it's not just skin colour, it's the shape of the body, and the way they do things.

They're loud. They're arrogant. I mean if I went to someone else's country I would treat it with respect. I would want to become part of how they do things, and, like, the parents did, but now, their kids they're just fucking arrogant. They go around playing music out their cars, all the fucking rap and shit.

Imagine if they did a scientific study and it found that black people were more stupid than white people – just like biologically. I read this on a website right? They wouldn't let that get out would they? It would be banned. They wouldn't even be able to do the study would they?

I bet they are. I bet they're all thick.

So you did her good Danny. Made her realise she should show some respect.

Good one.

Danny   Thanks.

Craig *puts his arm round* **Danny***'s neck affectionately.*

Krissie   I hurt.

Nurse   I'll get some more painkillers.

Krissie   Where's Gary?

Nurse   Who's Gary?

Krissie   My boyfriend. He was with me.

Nurse   There's been no one called Gary.

Krissie   Oh.

Oh.

I remember now.

Nurse   What?

Krissie   He left me.

Nurse   On the street.

Krissie   No he left me. We split up. Last night. Before it happened.

Nurse   So you were on your own?

Krissie   He was supposed to be walking me home.

Where is he?

Nurse   I don't know.

Krissie   At least you're here. You're very kind.

Nurse   It's my job Krissie.

Krissie   You know my name.

Nurse   It's on your notes.

Krissie   Are you going to look after me?

Nurse   For a day or two, yes.

Krissie   Are you a nurse?

Nurse   Yes.

Krissie   You don't look old enough to be a nurse.

Nurse   I'm twenty-one.

Krissie   I'm nineteen.

Nurse   I know.

Krissie   Oh. Notes.

What's your name?

Nurse   Patrick.

Krissie   I'm going to call you Angel.

Nurse   Don't you like Patrick?

Krissie   I think Patrick is lovely.

But Patrick is your name.

And I'm looking for a term of affection.

So Angel it is.

Nurse   Well I'll be Angel. And you can be Buffy.

Krissie   Great. Buffy. Vampire slayer. Brilliant.

Nurse   Maybe you've had enough painkillers?

Krissie   Maybe.

Danny *is working on the landfill.*

He looks up at the sky. He is numb.

He goes back to work.

His foot hits something on the ground.

He looks at it.

Uncovers something in the ground.

He digs it up. It is the knife.

He sits on the ground.

Craig   What's that?

I thought you buried it.

Danny   I did. But then there it was. Coming out of the ground. God.

Paul   What wrong with you?

Danny   It was a girl.

Raf   She didn't see us.

Danny   What about the police?

Raf   She doesn't know who we are.

Paul   So what about the police Danny?

Craig   It's alright, isn't it? Danny.

Danny   Yeah.

Paul   If you act weird, it's not good.

Danny

Paul   Not good for us is it?

Danny   No.

Paul   So what's this with the knife? Bury it.

Danny *stands up*.

Danny   I'm going.

Craig   Where?

Paul   Not with the knife.

Raf   You quitting?

Danny   Yeah. Yeah. I'm quitting.

Paul   Right.

Go on then, but if the police come looking, if I have to think about it again, or if I ever see you near here in the future, I'll break your fucking legs.

Cut you too.

Danny *goes.*

Craig   He won't go to the police.

He won't.

Gary   Did I just stand there because I'm a coward?

Or because I don't love her?

Or because I'm gay? And as we all know gay men don't . . .

Darren

Gary   Because I was guilty?

Because I don't believe God would allow it?

Because I don't believe in God.

And I wanted to teach her that?

Darren   You're not a bad person.

Gary   You're right not to be sure about that.

You're only saying that because for some reason you still love me.

Darren   You did a bad thing.

But you're not a bad person.

Gary   I want to hide.

Darren   That's not attractive. Go to the hospital. Sort it out.

Hayley's *front room.*

It is the morning after. The girls are still lying about.

Zara   He obviously liked you.

Hayley   You ever seen Natalie getting off with anyone?

Zara   Nah.

Carly   No.

Natalie   So?

Zara   Maybe she hasn't.

Hayley   Sixteen and never been kissed.

Carly   Oooo.

Zara   Ahhh. Well?

Hayley   Is that right? Nats? Is that true? You can tell us.

Natalie   I told you. There was that boy on holiday.

Hayley   Oh yeah, that boy on holiday. Right.

You're blushing Nats.

Just tell us the truth. Come on. We won't laugh. It's okay. It don't matter. Does it?

Natalie   Piss off.

Hayley   So you haven't then?

Natalie   No I haven't.

Alright?

Hayley   Okay.

Zara   Shit! Really?

Hayley   Zara.

Zara   Sorry.

Hayley   Why not?

Natalie   I don't know. No one wants to get off with me.

Carly   Do you want us to set you up?

Natalie   No.

Hayley   Why don't you call Danny tommorow, meet up and get off?

Natalie   He called me porky.

Hayley   Well yeah but . . .

Zara   He was pissed. He doesn't mean it. He likes you.

Natalie   I don't know.

Hayley   Text him now. Tell him you want to meet tomorrow.

Zara   Go on.

Zara *grabs* **Natalie***'s phone.*

Either you do, or I will.

Natalie   No . . . I'll do it.

What do I write?

Do you want to meet?

Hayley   Yeah. That's good. Then a massive load of kisses.

Zara   Er no? Just one little kiss at the end?

Natalie   Okay.

Shit.

I don't want to.

Hayley   What's the worst that could happen?

Natalie   Okay.

Send.

Shit.

Do you think he'll reply?

The girls nod.

Zara   Definitely.

Hayley   Come here.

Hayley *bounds over to* **Natalie** *and hugs her.*

Natalie's in love.

Natalie's gonna get a shag!

Nurse   So many flowers. Aren't you lucky?

Krissie   I was at a funeral, then attacked with a knife. I've got a cracked rib and a broken leg. I'm on painkillers, but I still hurt. My boyfriend, no, my ex-boyfriend has disappeared and left me to die.

And flowers give me hayfever.

Lucky?

Nurse   Yes. Lucky.

Krissie   I like your hair.

Nurse   Colour?

Style?

Shape?

Krissie   Smell. You use a scented shampoo. Don't you?

Nurse   That's a personal question.

Krissie   Are you gay?

Nurse   You assume I'm gay because I use a scented shampoo?

Krissie   Just asking.

Nurse   I'm not gay.

Krissie   Good.

Nurse   Why?

Krissie   Am I still attractive? Now that I'm . . .

Nurse You shouldn't ask me questions like that.

Krissie Boring.

*The **Nurse** whispers.*

Nurse Yes. You're beautiful.

But I never said it.

Harriet *comes in. She carries a bunch of flowers.*

Krissie I have a visitor.

*The **Nurse** leaves.*

Harriet Hi. Krissie?

Krissie Yeah. Hi.

Harriet I'm . . . Harriet?

Krissie Oh yeah. Right. You got me flowers.

Harriet Yeah.

Krissie Thanks.

I love flowers.

Harriet Good.

I wanted to say . . .

I'm sorry.

Krissie What for?

Harriet That . . . I couldn't stop them.

Krissie What?

Harriet I just watched. But . . . I could've got involved.

Krissie You did. You phoned for the ambulance. You tried to stop the bleeding.

That's more than enough.

Harriet Okay.

Krissie   Did you give the police a description?

Harriet   Of them? Last night? Yes.

Krissie   What did you tell them?

Harriet   Teenagers, male, white.

Krissie   What about the one who cut me?

Harriet   He was young. Fifteen, sixteen. Quite short.

Krissie   I didn't.

Harriet   What?

Krissie   I didn't give the police a description. I won't be pressing charges.

Harriet   Why not?

Krissie   I saw the boy that cut me before he did it. I heard them telling him to do it. I don't think he wanted to ... I think he was under pressure ... so I want to set an example. I want to forgive him.

And, this is difficult to ask, but I want you to do the same.

If the police ask for any more information, say no.

Harriet   Will they?

Krissie   They can prosecute without me. But they'll need you to testify.

Harriet   He cut you because you're ...

Krissie   What?

Harriet   You're ...

Krissie   What?

Harriet   You know.

Krissie   Short?

Harriet   Black.

Krissie   You think.

Harriet   Just saying, won't covering this up . . . send the wrong signals?

Krissie   I'm not covering it up. I'm worried this town has people who are waiting for an excuse to cause trouble. I don't want to give them that excuse. I want to give them a chance to stop. I'm trying to do what's right.

Harriet   Yes.

Krissie   I'm trying to find something good in this.

Harriet   I'll do whatever you want.

Krissie   Thank you.

Harriet   To forgive like that. It's not easy.

Krissie   Have you ever been in love?

Harriet   Yes.

I have been. Until . . . Yes.

Krissie   Well, no matter what that person did, however terrible, and however much you hated what they did, don't you think that somewhere in some place you would still love them? And eventually that might help you to forgive them.

Jesus said extend that.

Love everyone. Forgive everyone their sins.

Hate the sin, not the sinner.

Harriet   I'm not sure you can.

Krissie   Better to try though.

The **Nurse** *appears.*

Krissie   And maybe there's someone looking out for us.

Someone's sent me an Angel.

Danny *is waiting on the station platform. He has packed a bag, and is sitting on the metal seat.*

Tom *enters and stands for a moment.*

Then he sits down.

He starts to cry, trying to stop himself.

Danny *is embarrassed.*

Danny   You alright?

Tom   Yes.

Danny   Shut up then.

Tom *continues to cry.*

Danny   What's the matter?

Tom   I'm late.

Danny   Is that it?

Tom   I have to do this every day. Even though . . .

My girlfriend has walked out on me. And even though . . .

I'm suffering from clinical depression, and I've run out of pills. And . . .

I thought about killing myself this morning but I've been told if I'm late again, then I will face disciplinary action so I can't . . .

Danny   Where do you work?

Tom   London.

Danny   Is it good?

Tom   People hate each other. They only care about money, power, sex and their careers. No. It's not good. It's bad. Bad. You ever been?

Danny   Got a cousin in Ealing. That's where I'm going.

Tom   Don't.

Danny   My uncle had depression yeah? He kicked in a door at work, and they made him go to the doctor. He got signed off work for ages.

You should do that.

Kick in a door.

Tom   I'd lose my job.

Danny   Alright. Whatever.

Tom   What are you, fourteen? You don't have a clue. You don't know anything. Just play on your playstation or whatever.

Danny   Alright. Piss off then.

Tom   I'm a bastard at the moment.

The train arrives.

This is the London train.

Tom *stands up.*

Danny *reconsiders.*

Danny   I'll get the next one?

Tom   Sorry.

Danny *is looking away.*

Tom *gets on the train.*

Danny *gets a text message and gets his phone out.*

Jo, **Suze**, **Bryony** *and* **Ed** *are sitting around* **Krissie**'*s hospital bed.*

Ed   I know God's here with you Krissie.

Krissie   Yes.

Bryony   Will it . . . is it . . . ?

Krissie   Is it . . . ?

Bryony   Will it scar?

Krissie   There are things they can do . . . you know, plastic surgery.

Bryony   Oh right.

Jo   What about you? How do you feel?

Krissie   Sad.

Jo   About God.

Krissie   What?

Jo   You said you weren't sure about it before. When we said goodbye to Lilly.

Krissie   Oh. Yes. I know.

Jo   And then this happened.

Krissie   Yes.

Jo   So?

Krissie

Jo   Don't you think it's a message?

Suze   Jo.

Krissie   Do you?

Jo   We can't know for sure. But it seems . . .

Krissie   If there is a God – if I believe in any God, he doesn't *punish*. He forgives.

Suze   Of course.

Jo   But he could have stopped it happening, couldn't he?

Krissie

Jo   But he chose not to.

Suze   I don't think this is the right time to –

Jo   It's important she realises that God is here right now, all the time and he's powerful. He doesn't sit in the clouds. He was there when you said you didn't believe and he was there last night when this happened. Maybe you should accept that he's showing you a better way.

That's all I'm saying.

And you don't even know everything.

Ed   Jo.

Jo   What?

Ed   Stop it.

Krissie   What do you mean 'everything'?

Ed   We agreed she didn't have to know.

Jo   Maybe she should.

Ed   We agreed.

Jo   But maybe she should know.

Suze   Yeah. Come on. Jo.

Krissie   What?

Bryony   Krissie

Darren isn't at work.

He's with Gary.

Krissie   Is he looking after him? What happened?

Bryony   No. He's *with* Gary.

They're together.

I called him earlier and he told me.

They've been having a . . . relationship for a while.

Krissie   Oh.

Bryony   Sorry.

Ed   Yeah.

Jo   You see?

Krissie   Today just gets better and better doesn't it?

Harriet *is waiting in the hospital.*

Gary *enters.*

Sees **Harriet**. *They look at each other.*

Harriet   Hi.

Gary   Yeah.

How is she?

Harriet   She's got some friends in to see her now.

A cracked rib.

And a large scar across her face.

Her parents have gone home now. They'll come back at lunchtime.

They asked where you were. They said you were her boyfriend.

Gary   We split up.

Harriet   Not your problem then is it?

I told her parents I would wait. I think she needs someone to stay with her.

Where have you been?

Gary   At my boyfriend's.

Harriet   Oh.

Oh.

Does she know?

Gary   No.

Harriet   You going to tell her?

Gary   I was.

Harriet   Do you think that's a good idea? Right now.

Gary   I don't know.

Harriet   Why don't you *do* something instead?

Gary   Like what?

Harriet   She forgives the little twats who did this to her. She's not pressing charges.

Gary   She's not –

Harriet   She's not telling the police anything.

Gary   She's letting them get away with it?

Harriet   That's what she wants.

Gary   She's not thinking right.

Harriet   Maybe not but it's a small town isn't it?

What if you could find him?

The station platform.

Natalie   What you doing here?

Danny   I'm leaving.

Natalie   When?

Danny   Soon.

Natalie   I was glad you texted me.

Danny   Good.

Natalie   Who were those boys you were with?

Danny   Mates from work. Only just met them.

Natalie   Right.

They were twats.

Danny   Yeah.

Yeah, I'm sorry what I said. I was so wrong.

I was drunk. Really.

I like you. A lot. I think you're beautiful.

Natalie   Thank you.

Yeah.

I . . .

I like you.

I'm not very good at flirting.

But I like you.

A lot.

Danny   Thanks.

I want to kiss you.

Natalie   Oh.

Danny   Yeah.

Natalie   Now?

Danny   Yeah.

Natalie   Oh.

Danny   What?

Natalie   I . . .

I've never kissed a boy before.

Danny   Are you taking the piss?

Natalie   No.

Danny   What?

No?

Oh.

Okay.

Why not?

Natalie   No one wanted to.

Till now.

Is that okay?

Danny   Yeah.

But . . .

Shit.

I need to . . .

He shuffles away a little.

Shit.

Natalie   What is it?

She puts her hand out and touches his shoulder.

Danny   I . . . I want . . .

But . . .

Shit.

Natalie   What?

Danny *gets out the knife. Holds it.* **Natalie** *looks at it.*

Natalie   What you doing?

Danny   I know.

Natalie   Why have you got a knife?

Danny   I'm really sorry.

On Friday. The lads from work beat this girl up.

I was with them and they made me . . .

No . . . they told me I should cut her across the face.

Natalie   And? Did ya?

Danny   Yeah.

It was cos she was coloured. That's why we did it.

Cos she was black.

Natalie   You a racist then?

Danny   No.

Yes.

I suppose I must be.

Danny   I just ran away from work. Now I'm leaving. Going to London,

Natalie   Why?

Danny   I feel guilty.

Natalie   You're a psycho.

Are you gonna cut me?

Danny   No.

Natalie   Cos I'm white?

Danny   No. Because . . . I don't do that.

Natalie   I want to go.

Danny   Yeah.

Do you hate me?

Natalie   You're a racist and you cut up some girl in the face.

Danny   Yeah.

Natalie   Right then. I got my reasons.

Natalie *gets up.*

Stands for a moment.

Natalie   Listen yeah, you was gonna kiss me weren't you?

Danny   Yeah.

Natalie   Can we still do it?

So I can say I have?

Danny   But you hate me.

Natalie   Yeah. But, so I can say I have?

If you don't want to . . .

. . . then . . . .

Danny   No . . . I really want to.

Natalie   Okay.

Natalie *sits back down. They kiss.*

They finish and **Danny** *hugs her.*

He is upset.

Danny   I'm sorry.

Natalie *pulls away.*

Natalie   Thanks. Um . . . I'm not being funny, but you should tell that to the girl you cut. Not me. I don't want to see you again. You should give the knife to the police.

Danny   Bye.

Natalie *goes.*

Scene Four

Anthea, **James** *and* **Harriet** *are having coffee.* **Anthea** *and* **James** *are old school friends of* **Harriet**.

Anthea   You poor thing.

James   Chavs.

Anthea   Yeah. It's really not a nice place, is it?

James   It wasn't this bad when we were kids there. Was it? There weren't gangs of trevs with knives, attacking black people.

Anthea   When we were kids there weren't any black people.

James   A few.

Anthea   Maybe that's the reason it's got worse.

James   I think it's a little disturbing if you're suggesting that the introduction of a racial minority automatically causes a rise in violent crime.

Anthea   Of course I'm not saying that, not in the way that you're implying, I'm just saying that there may be more racial tension in the town now than there used to be.

James   It's just got more obvious. Come to the surface.

Anthea   You always do this to me, you always seem to suggest that my thoughts are in some way offensive. I think this is some kind of strange white middle-class guilt you have that we shouldn't talk about issues of race or poverty, because our lack of experience makes us intrinsically wrong, patronising and offensive. Which frankly is . . .

James   Not at all, but you can be a bit cavalier with your terminology.

Harriet   Do you think I should go back?

Anthea   What? To the hospital?

James   No. You've done your bit. Her family can look after her.

Harriet   To Tom.

Anthea   Oh. Tom? Look, you're being held back aren't you? I know you wanted this nice life, with a house, and a car, and a job and eventually a husband, but you're only twenty-two and you haven't done anything with that yet, have you?

James   Why don't you move away?

Harriet   It's home.

It's where I live.

Anthea   Come to London. Come visit.

Harriet   You could come here.

Anthea   It's nice to come back sometimes.

James   Sometimes.

Anthea   But it's boring. Isn't it?

James   And we'd probably get stabbed.

Harriet   So you think I should just leave him?

Anthea   He's pulling you down.

Krissie   When I'm better . . .

Um.

Nurse   What?

Krissie   Well I suppose I'm single again now so when . . .

Nurse   Yeah.

Krissie   Are you single Angel?

Nurse   Yeah.

Krissie   When I'm better, do you want to go for a drink?

Nurse   I can't answer that. I still have a professional duty to you.

Krissie   Oh.

Danny *looks up.*

Gary   It's you, isn't it?

Danny

Gary   Yeah.

Why did you do it?

Danny   I don't know.

Gary   Not enough.

Danny   I thought it would be good. I was pissed.

Gary   Not enough.

Danny   I was trying to impress people at work. I wanted to better myself.

Gary   What?

Danny   Drive the trucks.

Gary   You're a racist.

Danny   Yes.

Gary   You're an ignorant twat.

Danny   Yes.

Gary   You should be put down.

Danny   So hit me.

Gary   What?

Danny   Beat me up. Worse.

Go on. Please.

That's what you want to do?

Gary   Yeah.

Danny   So do it.

Gary   She's not pressing charges.

Danny   What?

Gary   She didn't even give them a description.

Danny   Oh.

Gary   So you'll get away with it.

Danny   That's why the police haven't . . .

Gary   Yeah. So . . .

Danny   So. Do it yourself. Hit me.

Or . . . did you bring a knife?

Gary   Yeah.

Gary *gets out a knife.*

Danny   Cut me then. I deserve it.

Gary   She forgives you.

Danny   What?

Gary   Yeah.

Danny   But . . . she . . .

That's . . . not enough.

Gary   What?

Danny   I don't want to be forgiven. I don't want . . .

. . . fuck . . .

Gary   She's gonna have a scar. Across her face.

Danny   Yeah. And she forgives me? Fuck.

Gary   She . . . you . . .

Gary *puts the knife away.*

You're a little shit.

Danny   I'm sorry. Yeah. I am. I'm sorry.

Gary   Tell that to her. Or just get on a train and fuck off.

Gary *goes.*

The girls have come out of school and are sitting in a playground.
Hayley *is on the phone to* **Natalie***.*

Hayley   We're on the swings mate. Yeah. Yeah. How'd it go?

Hayley *shares a smile with* **Carly** *and* **Zara***.*

Hayley   What?

Oh right.

Well come over here and tell us 'bout it?

Yeah.

Laters.

Hayley *hangs up and puts her phone away.*

Turns out he's a racist.

Carly   What that Danny?

Hayley   'parently he cut this black girl last night.

Zara   Bloody hell.

Hayley   Yeah.

But . . .

Natalie kissed him anyway.

Zara   What? Minging.

Carly   I wouldn't kiss a racist.

Hayley   Nah. I know. But she's . . . a bit, you know . . .

Carly   Yeah.

Hayley   Int she?

Carly   Yeah. Spose she is.

Zara   What?

Carly   Ugly.

Hayley   No. Lonely.

Carly   Right yeah. She's lonely.

Alright Natalie.

Natalie *has walked in. She sits down on the swing.*

Zara   You alright?

Natalie   No.

Zara   Right.

Hayley said you kissed a racist?

At least you've got off with someone now.

That's good.

Even if he is a psycho.

Natalie   I liked him. I think they made him do it.

Hayley   Alright, but don't go out with him Natalie cos he's mental.

Natalie   Maybe.

Carly   Does he have your number?

Natalie   Yeah. I texted him.

Carly   Oops.

Natalie   You told me to.

Zara   Was he a good kisser?

Natalie   Don't really know do I?

Zara   Oh yeah.

Natalie   You're . . .

You're sposed to put your tongue in yeah?

None of the girls look at her.

Yeah?

Hayley   Yeah.

I reckon.

Zara   Yeah. Probably.

Natalie   Don't you know?

Hayley   Yeah, but yeah, well it depends.

Natalie   On what?

Hayley   On . . . yeah . . . I . . . I don't know.

Natalie   Hayley, how many boys have you got off with?

Hayley   Can't remember.

Natalie   Zara?

Zara   Don't know. Not sure.

Natalie   Carly?

Carly   Twelve.

Natalie   Right.

But you two don't know?

Have either of you actually / ever got off with a boy?

Zara   Shut up. Yeah.

Hayley   It doesn't matter yeah?

I'd rather get off with no one than a racist.

Natalie   I don't think he's a racist.

Zara   Err. He cut a black girl with a knife? So . . .

Natalie   I think he would have cut anyone they told him to.

Zara   And you're saying that means he's not?

Natalie   I won't see him again. I know that.

Tom *is sitting in a chair. He is still in his suit from work. He is playing with a bowl of cereal.*

Harriet *enters.*

Harriet   I saw this attack in the street.

I stayed with the victim, this girl, in the hospital all night.

She's so brave. She forgives the people who did it.

Tom   You stayed with her, when she needed help. All night.

But you walk out on me.

Harriet   Yes.

Tom   I'm sorry.

I cut my arm this morning.

I haven't had a very good day.

The flat's a mess.

I think I've lost my job.

And I annoyed some kid at the station.

It's your fault though. You shouldn't have left.

Harriet

Tom   You can't love me.

Harriet   But I still do.

And I'm back.

And I'm staying. So get used to it.

And I think you want me to hug you.

Harriet *puts a hand out.* **Tom** *pushes it away, but* **Harriet** *is closer.*

Harriet *puts it out again.* **Tom** *pushes it away, but* **Harriet** *is closer.*

The same thing happens again, and now **Harriet** *puts both arms out and hugs* **Tom**. *He resists for a moment then relaxes.*

The hugs tighten.

Gary *enters and stands at the end of the bed.*

Gary   I'm sorry.

Krissie   For sleeping with someone else and not telling me?

Gary   Yes.

Krissie   Or leaving me to be knifed and running away?

Gary   Are you angry?

Krissie   Of course.

Gary   Do you hate me?

Krissie   No.

I love you. That's why I'm angry.

Gary   I was scared that if I went any closer they would stab me and that would be it. I couldn't move. I couldn't make my body move.

Krissie   I know. It was horrible. But before, why didn't you tell me you were seeing someone else. And after, why weren't you here to look after me?

Gary   I'm weak. Do you need anything?

Krissie   No.

Danny *walks in.*

Gary   This is Danny.

Krissie   Who's Danny? Another boyfriend?

Gary   Danny cut your face last night.

I found him at the station.

Krissie   How?

Gary   It's a small town.

Krissie   Yeah.

Hi.

Gary?

Gary   Yeah.

Krissie   You can go now.

Gary   But . . .

Krissie   Thank you for finding him. Now go away.

Gary *leaves.*

Danny   He said you forgive me.

Krissie   Yes.

Danny   Why?

Krissie   I heard them telling you what to do.

Danny   Yeah.

Krissie   You've not done anything like this before have you?

Danny   They said if I went to the police they would break my legs.

Krissie   These are your friends?

Danny   I don't want you to forgive me. You should have told the police. That's what they're there for. I should be in prison. I should be able to tell someone what I did and take what comes.

Krissie   I want to give you another chance.

Danny   It's not up to you. I did something wrong. You should just tell the truth.

Krissie   I'm sorry if I did the wrong thing.

What do you do?

Danny   What?

Krissie   Have you got a job?

Danny   I worked on the landfill. But I've quit.

Krissie   Did you like it?

Danny   I wanted to drive the trucks. But they made me just pick up stuff with a fork so it was crap.

Krissie   Why do you want to drive trucks?

Danny   Don't know.

Krissie   What do you want to be?

Danny   Better.

Krissie   What?

Danny   You know at school you'd fuck around and stuff. It was always me that got into trouble. I can't even do that.

Krissie   You got GCSEs?

Danny   One.

Krissie   In.

Danny   English. E. Did it early. Before I left.

Krissie   So you want a punishment? Get more. Then do A levels. Then a degree.

Danny   Can't afford it.

Krissie   Find a way.

Danny   I'm not clever enough.

Krissie   You knifed me because you thought it was important. You thought it was a way of being better. And you believed that because at the moment you're uneducated. You're not thick, but education gives you perspective. I'm a good person. I don't deserve to have a scar across my face because I'm black do I?

DO I?!

The **Nurse** *enters.*

Danny   No.

Krissie   So *don't* say you can't afford it. Don't say you're not clever enough. Think about me and my face. Think what you owe me. And when you've got your PhD and you're Doctor Danny you come back and show me.

Danny   It is difficult for me though. I don't have money and maybe my friends are twats but that's all I've got isn't it?

Krissie   You can –

Danny   But I will.

I'll do it.

I hope you get better soon.

Krissie   I hope you get better too.

Danny *goes.*

Nurse   Alright.

Krissie   Hello Angel.

Nurse   Want some good news?

You can go home later today.

Krissie   That is good news.

Nurse   That's not the good news.

Krissie   What then?

Nurse   I'm off duty tonight.

Krissie   Oh.

Are you?

Stuart *shows* **Danny** *into his office.*

Stuart   Come in.

Danny *comes in and sits down.*

Stuart   Right.

You told me you were going to work hard, but yesterday
you walked off the site in the middle of the day. Didn't tell
anyone.

I gave you a chance because I thought you need it but it
looks like I was wrong. So why have you come back?

Danny I came to apologise.

Stuart You can't have your job back.

Danny I'm going back to school. But I'm sorry I just left.
I should've done it all properly.

Stuart You're going back to school?

Danny Yeah.

Stuart Good.

How you going make money?

Can your mum afford you not to work?

Danny I'll find a way.

But I think you should know before I go that all of them,
they threatened me, they're racist, they're twats. They
scared the guy before off work.

Paul, Raf, Tyler, Craig.

Stuart I thought Craig was your mate.

Danny I thought you should know.

Stuart They're just lads. Mucking around.

Danny I've told you now.

Stuart Are you making some kind of complaint?

Danny No. I only worked here a day. But I thought you
might want to know.

Stuart I can't do anything Danny.

Danny *stands up.*

Danny   Paul Hughes said if I came back here, or if I told you, he would break my legs. He just saw me come in here, so I expect that's what he's going to do when I leave.

But I wanted to tell you.

Stuart   I'll keep an eye out. I'll listen. If I hear anything like what you're saying I'll fire them like a shot. But unless you want to make a formal complaint then there's not much I can do right now.

I hope your legs survive.

Danny   Yeah.

Stuart   Do you want me to call a taxi?

Danny   Can't afford it.

Danny *gets up and leaves the office.* **Paul**, **Raf**, **Craig** *and* **Tyler** *are there.*

Craig   Why d'you come back Danny?

Paul   It's gone half five. Time to clock off.

Shall we leave?

He looks at **Danny**.

After you.

Danny *walks off. The others follow him.* **Stuart** *watches.*

Sociologist   Ignorance is the enemy.

We must break down the imagined walls which surround these small towns and give these places community again. Rediscover the value of pride and purpose in . . .

She looks up.

In . . .

What are you doing?

Sit down.

She looks at her watch.

Oh. I've run over. Alright. Off you go then.

(*To herself.*) You don't care do you?

Lots of students grab their stuff and leave, chatting and happy.

Some hand things in to the **Sociologist**.

Almost last, **Danny** *comes down with a bag.*

Sociologist   Danny.

At least you were listening right?

Danny   It made me think.

Sociologist   That's the idea.

Danny   I walk around here, the city – the campus – and no one even looks at you. At least in a small town people have to deal with each other. They can't hide so they have to actually live *together*.

You missed that out.

He hands his essay to the **Sociologist**.

Thanks.

Danny *leaves.*

Sweetpeter

John Retallack and Usifu Jalloh

About the Authors

John Retallack was born in Oxford and is the founder and director of Company of Angels. He has written and directed a number of plays in recent years including *Risk* (2007), *Virgins* (2006), *Ballroom* (2004), *Club Asylum* (2002), *The Wild Girl* (2002), and *Hannah and Hanna* (2001). He was director of Oxford Stage Company from 1989 to 1999 and founding director of Actors Touring Company (ATC) from 1977 to 1985. He has toured and worked in many countries including Europe, India, Japan and America.

Usifu Jalloh from Sierra Leone is a professional actor, dancer, percussionist and storyteller. Since 1990 he has worked on numerous educational programmes in Sierra Leone, America and the UK. He has made two short films about refugees, including the award-winning *Journeyman* (2003).

About the Play

I wrote *Sweetpeter* because of a comment I read by Richard Weight in his book, *Patriots*, that 'in the English character liberalism and racism co-exist'. I knew something of Sierra Leone and thought that the story of that country embodied that observation. After all, the English abolished slavery, set up a colony there and called it 'Freedom' – and then, a century later, once again enslaved the very people that they had freed. The play was greatly helped in its composition through the collaboration with a great storyteller, Usifu Jalloh, who is himself a Sierra Leonian.

  Sweetpeter was produced by Company of Angels in association with Polka Theatre in September 2003, as part of a project called Young Europe. It toured the south of England and played at Polka Theatre for a season. There was a lot of dance in the play (choreographed by Landing Mane). The play has recently been translated into French by Severine Magois. The original cast was Lee Hart, Liza Hayden, Ewart James Walters, Leroy Liburd, Nina Kristofferson, with Sidney Smith in the title role of

Sweetpeter. This new version can be played without an interval and its running time is seventy-five to ninety minutes.

Characters

Sweetpeter, *aged between one day and twenty-one years*
His Father, *aged twenty-nine*
His Mother, *who is ageless*
**Gentlejesus/Mr Gentleman/Mr
   Gently/GentleKnight**, *various Englishmen*
**The Landlord/the Chief/the President/African
   Soldier**
A sixth part is taken by a professional musician.

In Act One, the action centres on the founding by English missionaries of 'The Land of Freedom', a colony on the west coast of Africa in the late eighteenth and nineteenth centuries. In Act Two, the action takes place in the period from Independence in 1961 and during the civil war in the late 1990s, concluding in present-day London.

Note: Modern dance was incorporated into the original production of *Sweetpeter*.

Act One

Scene One

Prologue: 1787

Sweetpeter (*a young African man in modern clothes*)
Sweetpeter is the story of me
and the story of my country,
the country where I lived and died,
lived and died . . .
The first time I was born
was not in my country,
but here, in England
on a ship moored in Deptford,
the *Victory*,
HMS *Victory*.
In my first life
I only lived one hour . . .

Indicates two slaves sitting either side of a bucket.

that's my father and my mother,
and the little bundle of joy
that she holds in her arms –
that's me.

Father Give me the boy.

Mother No I'll look after him.

Father Give me the boy. I want to hold him.

Mother No he's sleeping.

Father I want to hold him. He's my son.

Mother Let me keep him, he's asleep.

Father Give me the boy or I'll take him.

Mother I won't let him go.

Father Give me the boy.

Mother No.

They struggle and **Father** *snatches the boy.*

Father
My son will never be the son of a slave.
Better to lose a son
Than raise another slave.

Father *drowns the baby.* **Sweetpeter** *watches on, gasping for air.*

Scene Two

Gentlejesus *describes the treatment of slaves.*

. . .Then the local traders bring the slaves out, the biggest
first and a surgeon examines them to see that they are sound
of body.

Their greatest concern is to buy none that are diseased,
because they infect the rest.

When they have agreed what goods they will exchange for
them, they brand them on the arm with a hot iron, having
the letter of the ship's name on it.

After a week or more, it appears very plain and white on the
skin.

The slaves hate leaving their own country and will
sometimes leap out of the ship and into the sea, preferring
to drown rather than to depart.

Some are eaten by sharks.

Some will starve themselves to death even if they are flogged
for not taking the daily meal.

Some commanders cut off the legs or the arms of the most
stubborn to terrify the rest – this is one of the ways that the
European deals with savages.

It is a punishment so cruel that it haunts my sleep; it stops
my prayers.

The sea is sometimes rough for a whole week. Fevers break out and many slaves die.

When the weather is fine they let them all out of irons in the evenings so that they can air themselves.

The slaves jump and dance for an hour or two to the harp and fiddle to better preserve them in health . . .

It is the most barbaric custom I have ever seen.

I dedicate myself to the abolition of the accursed practice of slavery.

Scene Three

Mother *holds a tiny baby.*

Mother
My boy is a very clever boy, so versatile.
While his father held him down
Inside his blanket
Under the water,
He turned into a fish.
He swam around the bucket.
I lifted out my boy
Who was now a fish
And he turned straight back into
My little boy.
I was released from the ship.
They set me free
Because of him!
We have no money and I know nobody.
We sleep in the street.
Here we are –
Alive and free . . .
I am not a slave any more.

Mother *cuddles her son.*

Scene Four

Sweetpeter (*dressed as before*)
I've been
a fish a boy a bird a boy
a bat a boy
a lion
a boy a dog
and then a boy
who stays a boy

where I come from
life is short
and over quick
tic tic
tic tic
life is short
and over quick
tic tic
tic tic

you lose a life you find a life you lose another
you find a life you lose a life you find another
I was born with seven lives
And I've used six
Next time I lose a life
I won't get another
There'll be no one left
To love my mother

Scene Five

Sweetpeter's **father** *enters.*

Father
The family name is safe with me,
With me alone.
The job is done
I've killed my son.

No son need bear the shame
of a man who lives in chains.
I must lie down.
I hope that I will never wake again.

Scene Six

Gentlejesus (*to audience*)
The Land of Freedom is a most pleasant and fertile country
On the west coast of Africa.
On arrival a township will be marked out
And houses built by the joint labour of all
To provide immediate shelter.
Such is the mildness and fertility of the climate
That any kind of vegetable or grain will grow in the soil.
I am Gentlejesus, the clergyman who will accompany the
    pioneers.
They will receive instruction in the foundations of Christian
    belief,
English language, history and customs.
Strong alcohol, gambling and fornication outside marriage
Are forbidden.

Music begins.

Any black man or woman branded as a former slave
May sail to the newly founded Land of Freedom,
With free passage, food and cabin provided.

Mother *shows the brand on her arm.* **Gentlejesus** *speaks to*
Mother.

Please step aboard
Freedom waits.

Whole cast forms a ship sailing to the Land of Freedom.

Mother (*sings*)
    I looked over Jordan and what did I see?
    Coming for to carry me home

A band of angels coming after me
Coming for to carry me home

All (*sing*)

Swing low, sweet chariot
Coming for to carry me home
Swing low, sweet chariot
Coming for to carry me home

Mother

Me and my tiny son were destitute.
We sailed off to the Land of Freedom.
He was safe with me.

(*Sings.*)

If you get there before I do
Coming for to carry me home
Tell all my friends I'm coming too
Coming for to carry me home

All (*sing*)

Swing low, sweet chariot
Coming for to carry me home
Swing low, sweet chariot
Coming for to carry me home

Gentlejesus
Land ho!

Scene Seven

Gentlejesus *under an umbrella. He addresses the audience.*
Mother *sits to the side with* **Sweetpeter**.

Gentlejesus
My calling is
to bring the word of God to the heathen in Africa.
It is my duty to free the enslaved and to start a new world,
one in which white and black
are equal in the eyes of man,

as well as in the eyes of God.
I give my life to this calling;
It is why I have made the long and terrible voyage to Africa.
It has rained for three months –
Many slaves have not survived.
Perhaps I too will perish.
We have suffered great hardships.
Yet the gratitude the former slaves have shown to me
Makes good the Word of God,
Makes good the Word.
One day
We will build a cathedral in this place.

Mother (*holding baby*)
My boy has no father.

Gentlejesus
He is the child of our Lord.
He will always live in his loving care.

Mother
The rain is making him sick.
He has a fever.
It rains here all the time.
People are dying every day.
Soon there will be no one left.

Gentlejesus
Trust in the Lord.
The rain will cease and the sun will shine.
Remember our parable yesterday;
Forty days and nights,
Christ in the wilderness.

Mother
Still my boy is sick and he has no father.

Gentlejesus
Let us pray for him.

Mother
I am praying all the time.

I am praying now.
I want you to baptise my son.

Gentlejesus
Of course, my dear.
What is his name?

Mother
Slaves have no name.

Gentlejesus
What do you call him?

Mother
I call him 'Sweet'.

Gentlejesus
That's not a Christian name.

Mother
Please name my son, Father.

Gentlejesus
Luke? Paul? Peter?

Mother
Peter.

Gentlejesus
You are sure?

Mother (*pauses*)
Sweetpeter.

Gentlejesus
As you wish.
In the name of the Father, Son and Holy Ghost
I baptise thee 'Sweetpeter'.

He touches the baby's head with water.

Mother (*to* **Gentlejesus**)
Thank you for baptising my son.

To audience.

That same day
My boy died for the second time.
He was only six months old.

Sweetpeter became a bird.
He flew between the palms,
Through the forests and over the green hills,
To places where the sun shines all day.

Music. **Sweetpeter** *becomes a bird.*

Perhaps he went to heaven,
But he never said.
Sometimes, he brought me fruits and berries,
Sweet gifts –
And flew away again.
He was a beautiful bird.
Then he stopped coming.
He was lost to me.
This time he almost broke my heart.
Gentlejesus was kind.
He taught me to read
And I sang hymns.

Mother *sings 'All Things Bright and Beautiful'. She reads from the New Testament with* **Gentlejesus**. **Mother** *reveres* **Gentlejesus** *and his teachings.*

Scene Eight

Sweetpeter (*now dressed as a boy, appears as bird/lyrical image*)
Africa looked beautiful from above;
When I soared high it looked like paradise.
This was freedom.
But there was no one to share it with!
After I don't know how long
I missed my mother and I flew down to find her.

He shits on the missionary's head, who jumps up and feverishly pats his pate. **Sweetpeter** *the bird lands between his* **Mother** *and* **Gentlejesus**.

Mother
Go away, bird!

Sweetpeter
It's me!

Mother
Ugly bird, go away!

Sweetpeter
Mother it's me!

Mother
Sweetpeter my child!
I'm happy to see you again –
It's so very lonely without you!
Gentlejesus is teaching me.

Sweetpeter
What is he teaching you, Mother?

Gentlejesus
The Son of God was a humble man like you or I,
A humble man who loved everyone
Regardless of race or the colour of a man's skin.
He loves you, Sweetpeter.

Sweetpeter
How does he know me?

Gentlejesus
He is everywhere.

Sweetpeter
Where is he now?

Gentlejesus
He is here.
And he is not here

Sweetpeter
Are you Jesus?

Gentlejesus
I am the Word of Jesus.
He is the Light of the World.

Sweetpeter
Does he live in England?

Gentlejesus
Yes, he does.
Jesus is in England.
And he is everywhere.
He is in our hearts.

Sweetpeter
You are Jesus?

Gentlejesus
I am the Word of Jesus.
That is different.
In the beginning was the Word.

Sweetpeter
Jesus loves me?

Gentlejesus
He loves you.
You are his son,
The son of Jesus.

Sweetpeter
He is my father?

Gentlejesus
He is your Holy Father.

Sweetpeter
What is 'Holy'?

Gentlejesus
'Holy' is perfect.

Sweetpeter
But can he see my own father?

Gentlejesus
Of course he can.

Sweetpeter
I can't see him.

Gentlejesus
Jesus is your father too.

Sweetpeter
Can Jesus see my own father?

Gentlejesus
If your father can see Jesus,
Then Jesus can see your father.

Sweetpeter
I don't know where my father is
And neither does my mother.

Gentlejesus
Trust in Jesus to find him.
Love Jesus as he loves you.
Let us pray.

Sweetpeter
What is pray?

Gentlejesus
Down on your knees, boy, and repeat after me.

Gentlejesus *speaks the Lord's prayer.* **Sweetpeter** *repeats it in Krio.*

We papa god widin-a 'eaven
We respec you name
Make you wold come
We go do you work na dis wol
Just lik na 'eaven
Gi we ting fo eat tiday
And forgive we we sin

Just lik how we do forgive them when we sin 'pon we
Make we no go pon temptation
Pull we com out pon trouble
De wol na you y'own
You power e' you glory
Tene nang
Amen.

Gentlejesus (*to audience*)
Many have treated the black man as having no mind.
Many have denied him a soul.
The Christian church today believes he has both.
The Land of Freedom shows how passionately
We support this new understanding.

Mother (*sings*)
There's gonna be freedom
There's gonna be freedom
Oh, freedom
When Jesus comes

All (*sing*)
First there'll be no separation
There'll be no segregation
There'll be freedom
When Jesus comes . . .

Dance: Freedom develops into a small society that functions happily.

Scene Nine

Sweetpeter's father
Time passes –
But not for me.
I grow not one day older
Than the day I killed my son.
When I stop for long in one place –
My dreams become so bad,
I try to kill myself.

When I fire, the gun jams –
When I jump from the roof,
I float to earth –
God's punished me with life.

I build railroads.
I sail the seas in a cargo boat.
I work in places where all black faces
Are hated and despised.
'He may be a heathen nigger,' they say,
'But man, this boy can work!'
Sometimes they offer me a bigger wage,
But always I say,
'Sorry – no – must keep movin' on'. . .
I work where work means moving on,
Movin' on.

Dance ends here with **Father** *walking around the world.*

Scene Ten

Mother (*to audience*)
My son speaks English.
He is top of his class in most subjects,
English, English history, Bible study, geography.
He says he's found a father in Gentlejesus.
I thank Gentlejesus for his kindness and his inspiration,
I thank him from the bottom of my heart.
My boy has lost all fear.
He speaks the word of the Lord to all who wish to hear
And he speaks so well –
He's the first to speak the gospel in Krio,
He converts a whole village in a single afternoon.
Gentlejesus cannot believe it.
He says it would take him several lifetimes
To save so many souls as Sweetpeter.

Sweetpeter *delivers the nineteenth-century parable of Bishop Aggrey, one of the first west African bishops.* **Sweetpeter** *performs this short parable with practised gestures in an exciting mix of Krio and*

English. It is a very different style to that of Gentlejesus, though the message is the same and learnt entirely from the missionary. He is proud to be watched by **Gentlejesus** *and his* **Mother**.

Sweetpeter
A certain man went walking through the forest,
seeking any bird of interest he might find.
He came across a baby eagle.
He decided to take this eagle home.
He would raise it among his chickens, his ducks and his
    turkeys.
Five years later, a naturalist was passing through his garden.
He saw this eagle, king of birds, feeding amongst the
    chickens.
He turned and he says to the farmer,
'Farmer, dis na eagle, king of birds, not o common chicken.'
'Yes,' said the farmer, 'but I've raised him like a common
    chicken.'
'No, just give me chance, and I gon' make this eagle fly.'
The naturalist picked the eagle up, and he said,
'Eagle, you na eagle, now fly!'
Not knowing what to do,
the eagle looking this way and that way,
this way and that way,
seeing the chickens, the ducks and the turkeys feeding,
also jumps down and feeds with them.
'You see!' said the farmer, 'this na common chicken, not o
    eagle.'
'No!' said the naturalist, 'just give me chance and I gon'
    make this eagle fly.'
So the next day,
he took the eagle to the top of the house.
This time he said to the eagle,
'Eagle, you na eagle, now fly!'
Once again, not knowing what to do,
the eagle looks this way and that way,
this way and that way,
finally, seeing the chickens feeding,
also jumps down and feeds with them.

'You see!' said the farmer, 'this na common chicken, not o
    eagle.'
'No!' said the naturalist, 'it is an eagle, it has the heart of an
    eagle,
just give me one more chance and I gon' make this eagle
    fly.'
So the next day, he took the eagle away from the houses,
away from the city to the top of a high mountain,
just as the sun was rising.
And once again he said to the eagle,
'Eagle, you na eagle, now fly!'
Upon seeing the beautiful valleys in the distance before it,
the eagle began to shake,
shake as if a new life had come to it, but did not fly.
So the naturalist turned the eagle's head
and made it face the beauty and the glory of the morning
    sun.
All of a sudden, without warning, and with a mighty
    screech,
the eagle spread its wings and lifted higher and higher
into the sky and did not return.
It was an eagle,
it had the heart of an eagle and
it will always remain an eagle,
even though it had been kept and tamed as a chicken.
So people, I put it to you:
focus your eyes on the light of the world.
Focus your eyes on Jesus, and
He will make you fly!

Mother
The people love Sweetpeter and all that he says to them.
The chiefs in the villages are a different matter.

Chief (*to* **Sweetpeter**)
You idolise the white Jesus;
now the people of my village idolise Jesus too.
They all want to fly from the top of the mountain.
There are no chickens left in my village!

Everyone is an eagle now!
I wish you had never come to my village
and I wish you had never talked to my people.
I ask you please leave, and never return.

Mother
I am sure Gentlejesus will encourage my son!

Gentlejesus
Sweetpeter, thank you.
An interesting experiment.
In future, however, you must spread the gospel in English,
in its glorious original language,
that of the St James Bible.
Please don't be discouraged
But if I, Gentlejesus, can't follow all you say,
I am reluctant to baptise hundreds of people in a single
    afternoon!
We needs must take the authentic route,
'The Slow Road'.
We will build our congregation day by day.

Sweetpeter
But –

Gentlejesus
Bless you, my son.

Sweetpeter
I don't know who I am any more.
Some call me a Black Englishman
Others a White African.
I love you, Mother.

Music / **Sweetpeter** *departs.*

Mother
He's disappeared!
I don't know where to find him or how to call him.
He's just gone,
Gone off to the natural world –
Gone to a place where he can be

Anything he wants to be.

Enter **Sweetpeter**.

He's become a bat
And hangs upside down at night
On the cotton tree
In the centre of our town.
He hadn't realised that bats are blind
So it took him years to find me again.

Sweetpeter *crashes into the wall and exits.*

All around him,
All around the cotton tree,
The town of Freetown grew.
The town became a city.
All of us,
African and European,
Lived and worked together
In prosperity and in harmony.
We traded, we studied and we prayed –
We built a new kingdom here on earth.
I wished my boy could see how beautiful
Our city had become.
But he couldn't see it,
He couldn't see the city grow.
He couldn't see the new Freetown,
Our Freetown!

1860: Dance of Freetown. The town becomes a city, a melting pot of peoples, a trading port. The dance incorporates shouts and cries in different languages. It is joyous, ebullient and optimistic.

Scene Eleven

At the climax of the dance, **Sweetpeter** *enters and joins his* **Mother**. *She is overjoyed.*

Mother
Sweetpeter! My boy!
Oh bless his darling heart,
He wants to start again!
Oh Sweetpeter, I am so happy to see you again!
What brought you back to me?

Sweetpeter   I missed you, Mother.

Mother   My darling son!

They reunite.

(*To audience.*) I'll bring him up even better
Than I brought him up before!
I'll teach him to read, to walk, to write, to be polite –
He'll be as good a man as you can find in Freetown.
He'll get a proper job.
He'll make his mother proud.

Music: **Mother** *dresses* **Sweetpeter** *in an English-style school cap and tie.*

He goes to Queen Victoria College
The best school in Freetown,
In my humble opinion.
And he has the best teacher,
Mr Gentleman.

Mr Gentleman *enters. He is elegant, confident and precise. Following display of knowledge happens at an electrifying pace.*

Mr Gentleman   Sweetpeter, name the counties . . .

Sweetpeter   Bedfordshire, Berkshire, Buckinghamshire, Cambridgeshire, Devonshire, Derbyshire, Durham, Essex, Gloucestershire, Herefordshire, Huntingdonshire, Kent, Lancashire, Leicestershire, London, Monmouthshire, Northamptonshire, Nottinghamshire, Rutlandshire, Shropshire, Somersetshire, Sussex, Warwickshire, Wiltshire, Yorkshire, Sah!

Mr Gentleman   Name the kings and queens of your country . . .

Sweetpeter   Of England?

Mr Gentleman   Of course, boy!

Sweetpeter
Henry VII,
Henry VIII,
Edward VI,
Mary I,
Elizabeth I,
James I,
Charles I,
Oliver Cromwell!
Charles II
James II,
William and Mary jointly,
William III,
Anne,
George I,
George II,
George III,
George IV,
William IV,
Queen Victoria,
Sah!

Mr Gentleman   Name five great women in recent history.

Sweetpeter   Florence Nightingale, Elizabeth Fry, Marie Curie, Mary Livingstone, Queen Victoria, Sah!

Mr Gentleman   Name ten different types of garden bird.

Sweetpeter   In England?

Mr Gentleman   Of course, boy!

Sweetpeter   Pigeon, sparrow, finch, magpie, starling, blackbird, swallow, flamingo and ostrich –

Mr Gentleman   – of England!

Sweetpeter   – blue tit and red robin, Sah!

Mr Gentleman
Shakespeare, Sweetpeter?

Sweetpeter
'To be or not to be, *dis na de question*
whether e' better for suffer na you mind
de wahalla pon bebe rebe gentegi
o' for fete de wahalla in donam
for die, an no sleep again
an if we sleep, we don de plenty 'eartache
and de plenty trouble da de flesh tout.'

Mr Gentleman   English, Sweetpeter!

Sweetpeter
'Tis a consummation
devoutly to be wish'd, to die to sleep,
to sleep, perchance to dream . . . *Sah*!

Music: **Mr Gentleman** *and* **Sweetpeter** *don boxing gloves in unison. They spar and are evenly matched.* **Sweepeter** *gets the last punch. They touch gloves to finish.* **Sweetpeter** *takes off gloves.* **Sweetpeter** *and* **Mr Gentleman** *sing 'Hearts of Oak' together.*

Till Britain shall triumph our ships shall plough to sea,
Our standard be justice, our watchword be free!
Then cheer up, my lads, with one voice let us sing,
Our soldiers, our sailors, our statesmen and King.
Hearts of oak, our ships,
Hearts of oak, our men.
We always are ready,
Steady, boy! Steady!
We'll fight and we'll conquer again and again.

Mother *dresses him in the same clothes that* **Mr Gentleman** *wears;* **Sweetpeter** *and the teacher are now both dressed the same.* **Mr Gentleman** *awards* **Sweetpeter** *a silver cup.*

Mr Gentleman   Well done, Sweetpeter! You have come out top of the school!

Mr Gentleman *and* **Sweetpeter** *shake hands.*

Mr Gentleman   You must be a very proud mother, I am sure.

Mother   Thank you thank you thank you sir.

Sweetpeter *is looking at his feet.*

Mr Gentleman   Are you alright boy?

Mother (*to* **Mr Gentleman**)
He's alright, sir.
He has no father to tell of his success.
He is always a little jealous of the other boys
When he does well.

Mr Gentleman
He is an outstanding student,
An example to one and all.

Mother
You have been a father to him, Mr Gentleman.
Is that not right, Sweetpeter?

Sweetpeter *looks up and nods and looks at* **Mr Gentleman**.
They shake hands. **Sweetpeter** *impulsively embraces his teacher.*
Mr Gentleman *steps back from the embrace.*

Mr Gentleman   If you will excuse me?

Mr Gentleman *exits.*

Sweetpeter   Mother!

Mother   Yes Sweetpeter?

Sweetpeter   I know what I want to be.

Mother   What's that, Sweetpeter?

Sweetpeter   I want to be a teacher!

Mother   That's a very good thing for a boy like you to be.

Sweetpeter   I can be anything I want to be!

Mother   That's right!

Dance of mother and son. This the peak of their optimism for the future. **Sweetpeter** *receives his hat and his brolly and his buttonhole.* **Mother** *dotes on her boy and he basks in her light.*

Scene Twelve

Prize-giving and Speech Day.

Sweetpeter
The school insists the new African teachers dress like this.
There's only a few of us.

Mother
You look wonderful my son.
I am sure that you will be a great teacher.
Congratulations Sweetpeter.

Here in Freetown
The African is equal to the Englishman.
That's why he lets you wear his clothes.

They sit on the floor to listen to the speeches.

Mr Gentleman
Thank the Lord
Slavery is now in the past.
We live together in a country where all men are free.
We believe that the native African
Is free to live in his native country,
as he did before the curse of slavery,
as he has done so since time immemorial.

Applause.

Europeans believe passionately in
the right of the African to his land
and to his heritage.
Thus we say to you –

let the European sit at the desk,
let the European toil through the night
over the details of your laws and your accounts.
Let the European do the thinking
and you, you the proud African,
you do the living!

Applause.

In line with this radical and progressive thinking,
the school committee at Victoria College
has requested me to ask you
one simple but profound question:
How can we ask Free Men
to teach subjects that they know nothing about?
We, the Europeans, have, I fear,
been idealistic at the expense of you,
you, the African.
Henceforward, at Victoria College
and at schools throughout the country,
all European subjects will be taught only by Europeans.
Voice-over with tannoy effect, as if a public decree. **Sweetpeter**
slowly rises and steps behind gauze. **Mother** *gently assists him to
remove all his clothes. During the following, he puts on an old pair of
shorts and a torn short-sleeved shirt.*

'The government decrees that it is no longer advisable to
employ natives of west Africa as doctors, lawyers,
administrators, teachers, or in any other advanced
professional capacity that requires higher levels of
education. The government does not believe the
professional capacities of the west African professional to be
on a par with the European professional. The above decree
becomes effective from midnight tonight.'

Scene Thirteen

1900: **Sweetpeter** *is now dressed like a poor houseboy.* **Mr
Gentleman** *sits down in a wicker chair and puts his feet up.*

Mr Gentleman   Boy!

Sweetpeter   Sah!

Mr Gentleman
You work from Monday to Monday
January to January
Six a.m. to midnight
Stay clean
No reading
No writing
Don't marry
Don't change
Don't grow.
Alright boy?

Sweetpeter   Sah!

Mr Gentleman   Sir!

Sweetpeter   Sah!

Mr Gentleman
Sir!
I will pay you a shilling a month
Full board
And if you must visit the doctor
I'll look after that.

Sweetpeter   What are my duties, Sah?

Sweetpeter *stylises the following tasks.*

Mr Gentleman
Clean my shoes
Pour my gin
Make my bed
Clean the toilet
Wash the floor
Darn my socks
Iron my shirts
Bring my tea
Guard the house

Walk the dogs
Dust my books
You'll soon get the hang of it
Go away.

Sweetpeter   Sah!

Mother
My poor son!
He's been a fish and a bird and a bat –
But this time he's lost the will to change.
He stayed a houseboy for fifty years.

She gently touches the (now docile) **Sweetpeter** *on the arm.*

You are going to have to start again, Sweetpeter.

Sweetpeter   What do you mean?

Mother *hands him a piece of chalk.*

Mother   Write your name.

Sweetpeter   I've forgotten my name.

Mother *writes it on the floor.*

Mother   There!

Sweetpeter *stares at it and tries to decipher it.*

Sweetpeter   What does it say?

Mother   It says your name: 'Sweetpeter'.

Sweetpeter   Sweet. Peter.

Mother
Say it again.
It might be a long time before you hear it again.

Sweetpeter   Sweetpeter…

Mother *gently embraces* **Sweetpeter**. *They turn to audience as joint narrators of the story.*

Sweetpeter *and* **Mother** (*to audience*)
In Europe,
Time moves forward
But here, in Freetown,
That is only one of the moves
Time makes.
It stops sometimes for years
Or goes backwards
Or does a little dance and doesn't know
Which way it's going.
We think time moves forward –
Then we look to the side and see
It doesn't move at all.
We've been here before!
We're not going backwards or forwards –
We're just repeating things.
Look!
We're slaves again!

Sweetpeter *and* **Mother** *are chained by* **Mr Gentleman**.
Sweetpeter *turns back into a bird.*

Act Two

Scene One

1961: **Mother** *is sitting on a chair with an old radio to which she is listening.*

Voice-over   Today the Country of Freedom becomes a unified and independent nation to take her place as an equal partner in the Commonwealth of Nations and as an entity in the world at large.

I ask you to deal fairly and honestly with your fellow men, to discourage lawlessness, and to strive actively for peace, friendship and unity in our country . . .

Scene Two

Music: Dance of Independence. **Mother** *is in the centre. The bird appears and* **Sweetpeter** *materialises.*

Mother   How did you know that this is The Day?

Sweetpeter   I heard the singing from above the clouds and I flew down and I saw thousands of people around the cotton tree in the middle of the city – I saw you there and I landed on its branches –

The president comes by in his car.

Mother
Look! The president! Can you believe your eyes?
An African is the leader and the father of us all!

Sweetpeter   I want to serve him.

Mother   I want that too!

Sweetpeter   I will be president myself one day.

Mother   Now you can really be anything you want to be!

Sweetpeter
Yes, Mother! But not only me!
We can all be anything we want to be!

Dance finishes.

Scene Three

Sweetpeter's father.
I was a soldier for a century.
I fought for the British in the trenches,
on the beachheads,
in Korea and Argentina.

Moving on,
I came home at last.
There was so much work for me here –
In Africa.

I am a mercenary.
My heart has turned to stone.
I'm hard and as old as hell.
Bombs shatter and fire burns –
but always I survive.

I report for duty every day,
a legend to all who serve me.
I'm Mistah Mistah.
That's how they know me.

Two centuries ago, I had a name,
a wife, a son.
I forget their faces, I forget their names,
I don't even know my own.

I must keep moving on,
moving on.

Scene Four

Music: 'System Dread'. **Mother** *radiant in polka-dot dress.*
Sweetpeter *helps* **Mother** *wheel a little street bar with beer and
nuts and a national flag at the top of it to keep off the sun.*
Sweetpeter *goes off to get more beer. The bar has an eighteen-inch
statue of Gentlejesus on it to whom she speaks.*

Mother (*to Gentlejesus statue*)
When first I sailed to Freedom
the advertisement stated,
'Strong alcohol, gambling and fornication outside marriage
    are forbidden.'
Things have changed a lot since then.
There are no rules any more!
The president spends all the people's money
on himself and his family.
Many people want to kill him, Lord.
He say everyone love the president.
But no one loves him, Lord –
if we say we don't love him, we get beat up, or worse.

She eyes a man coming up to the bar.

Everyone thinks they are the president now,
even the landlord.

Come here Sweetpeter!

Sweetpeter *enters.* **The Landlord** *enters and sits down with*
Mr Gently. **Mr Gently**, *a dealer in precious stones, wears a
short-sleeved French suit. Both carry briefcases. The* **Landlord**
invites **Mr Gently** *to sit down with him.*

The Landlord (*to* **Mother**)   Haven't I told you not to
play that stupid jamba-smoking drug music in here? Now
bring me two beers!

Sweetpeter *brings beers.*

The Landlord   What's this? Where are the glasses for the
beer? (*To* **Mr Gently**.) I have the necessary contacts.

Mr Gently Is that so?

The Landlord Oh yes! I know everyone, everyone worth knowing that is!

Mr Gently You have actual connections with the president himself?

The Landlord With the president himself!

Mr Gently Can I ask – I mean – are you related or just friends?

The Landlord Both actually. The president and me go back a long way. Drinking partners you can say! The president's sister-in-law is a close friend of my wife. I can help you to avoid tax and export duty.

The dealer looks down at the table. **Sweetpeter** *returns with glasses.*

The Landlord What is the matter with you bobo? Do you expect my guest to sit down at a dirty table?

Sweetpeter Sorry Sah, I –

The Landlord Shut up! We have an important meeting now!

Sweetpeter *wipes.*

The Landlord (*to* **Sweetpeter**) Do you think I just keep you here to feed you and your mother?

Sweetpeter No Sah.

The Landlord (*to* **Mr Gently**) Please sit down. Don't mind the mess. These boys are sometimes very useless. All they are good at is stealing, begging, eating and anything unprogressive. You have to be careful – strike first. I'm always prepared.

He taps the gun in his soft briefcase.

You too?

Mr Gently   Of course.

The Landlord   Are you hungry? Would you like some nuts? (*Shouts to bar.*) I want a selection of nuts!

Mother *puts bowl of nuts on the table.*

The Landlord   You don't know how to say good afternoon any more? Don't you know how to show respect? Get out from my sight, useless thing!

Mother *ignores him and walks to bar.*

The Landlord (*to* **Mr Gently**)   I am sorry I am not normally like this. But when you have a woman who is as uncivilised as this one, you have to be strong, eh? Show who is boss, ay?

Mr Gently   Is this bar yours then?

The Landlord   This is only one of my bars. I've got a dozen in the city – each one with a hostess. I'll look after you, Mister Gently. You like women, my friend?

Mr Gently   I'm not averse.

The Landlord   You like African woman?

Mr Gently   I've never . . . well, I –

The Landlord   You like her?

Mr Gently   Well. I couldn't fail to notice her, she's very attractive, but –

The Landlord   Enough my friend – you are at the City Hotel?

Mr Gently   That's right.

The Landlord   She is exclusively under my control. Two more beers! Boy!

Sweetpeter *takes beers from his* **Mother** *and serves them.*

Mr Gently   Let me.

The Landlord   You are my guest, Mister Gently. What kind of investment are you considering? What type of stone?

Mr Gently *looks slightly anxious as if he might be overheard.* **The Landlord** *looks amused.*

The Landlord   They are not educated, Mr Gently. They have not got a business studies degree from the University of Birmingham. They are morons.

He stares at **Sweetpeter** *and* **Mother**. *They stare back at him.*

(*To* **Mr Gently**.) How much?

Mr Gently   That depends. There's a minimum, but no maximum . . .

Lights change to **Sweetpeter** *and* **Mother**.

Sweetpeter   I'll kill him!

Mother   Calm down, calm down –

Sweetpeter   He talks about you like you a prostitute! He thinks he can give you to anyone he likes – and you say nothing –

Mother   Do you want me to beg?

Sweetpeter   This is no better!

Mother   Do you want me to beg?

Sweetpeter   Is there nothing else you can do?

Mother   I'll talk to him – he was just sounding big – he didn't mean what he said – he didn't mean it, I'm sure – please don't say anything to him.

Sweetpeter   Mother, I can't let him talk like that, he's a pig –

Mother   Please don't or he will throw us out.

Sweetpeter   Let him throw us out – I'd sooner be on the street than here!

Mr Gently *exits*. **The Landlord** *returns*. **Sweetpeter** *hides*.

The Landlord You are here to serve me and my guests – to provide whatever makes us comfortable.

Mother Of course sir, I'm sorry.

The Landlord Sorry? What is sorry? Sorry is an easy little word, anyone can say sorry. I am your landlord, I am your boss, you do anything I ask, you understand?

Mother Yes sir.

The Landlord Yes sir, what?

Mother I understand sir.

The Landlord And you keep that heathen boy under control. D'you hear? He's not polite, he hasn't got respect.

Mother I will tell him.

The Landlord You must give him discipline. He needs a father to curb him

Mother Yes sir.

The Landlord I don't like it when you don't greet me, and don't show respect when I have Europeans here. You understand?

Mother Yes sir.

The Landlord Come here. I've got a job for you. Come here.

He tries to kiss her and she resists him. He strikes her hard and she falls to the ground. **Sweetpeter** *enters with a machete.*

Sweetpeter Get out pig!

The Landlord Stay where you are, boy.

Sweetpeter Get out pigman!

Mother Do what he says Sweetpeter!

The Landlord I warned you!

Sweetpeter *lunges at him.* **The Landlord** *shoots him pointblank.* **Sweetpeter** *drops to floor.* **Mother** *screams. He holds the gun to her head.*

The Landlord   Stand up! You are not going to tell anyone about this accident, are you?

Mother   No sir.

The Landlord   Do you know why you are not going to tell anyone?

Mother   No sir.

The Landlord   Because there is no one to tell. No one is interested, not even the president. And don't bother to call the police – they are my good friends. Now come here.

She pulls away and runs to **Sweetpeter**'s *body. She whispers to her son.*

Mother   Do your magic, boy, and run from this place. There's no one worth staying here for, not even for your mother. I have lost my worth.

The Landlord *drags* **Mother** *off. Music.* **Sweetpeter** *transforms into a lion.*

Scene Five

The lion stalks and leaps, roaring. **Father** *enters with a rifle. He calmly shoots the lion. The lion stumbles and dies.* **Sweetpeter** *is transformed into a young rebel soldier. He is given new clothes and trainers.* **Father** *hands* **Sweetpeter** *a gun.* **Father** *controls this slick routine.* **Sweetpeter** *takes on the swagger of the boy soldier.*

Father
Kill your parents.

Sweetpeter
What?

Father
Kill your parents.

Sweetpeter
I can't do that.

Father
If you don't kill your parents,
I'll kill you.

Sweetpeter
My mother's dead.

Father
If you're lying boy,
I'll cut out your tongue.

Sweetpeter
And I don't have a father.

Father
Everyone has a father.

Sweetpeter
Not me.
I never saw my father.

Father
If you're lying boy,
I'll cut off your hand.

Sweetpeter
I'm not lying.

Father
What is your name?

Sweetpeter
I was born with no name.

Father
What do they call you?

Sweetpeter
Sweetpeter.

Father
Who gave you that name?

Sweetpeter
Gentlejesus.

Father
Where does he live?

Sweetpeter
He lives in my church.

Father
Kill him.

Sweetpeter
Kill Gentlejesus?

Father
You heard.
Say it!

Sweetpeter *shakes his head.*

Father
I can't hear you!

Sweetpeter (*in a whisper*)
Kill Gentlejesus.

Father
That's better boy.
Can you fight?

Sweetpeter
I want to fight.

Father
Can you shoot?

Sweetpeter
I want to shoot.

Father
Can you read?

Sweetpeter
I used to read and I used to write and I used to speak so
beautifully that people cried and wanted me to speak the
Word all over again.
I worshipped Gentlejesus with all my heart and those people
to whom I spoke, they worshipped me.
I was going to be a preacher – but they said no.
Then I learnt many things, many names and numbers and I
spoke the words of Hamlet and I sang and I danced and
I boxed.
I was going to be a teacher – but they said no.

Father
Put down the gun.
Hold this.

Father *brings forward a crate, and a machete and he places a
watermelon upon it.*

Take careful aim.

Sweetpeter
Then I cleaned the arse of the white man for half a century.
I couldn't remember who I was.
I forgot my own name.

Father (*indicates melon*).
This is white boss

Sweetpeter *grips the machete.*

Sweetpeter
Then my mother and me got Independence.
We got our freedom!
Then they took it away again.

Father (*indicates melon*).
This is the president

Sweetpeter *raises the machete.*

Sweetpeter
Then the man who owned our room and our bar
Killed me – and raped my mother!

Father (*indicates melon*).
This is the landlord.

Sweetpeter *raises the machete higher.*

Sweetpeter
And no one ever came to help my mother
Or to help me.

Father (*indicates melon*).
This is your father.

Sweetpeter *brings down the machete in one powerful move with a terrible scream.* **Father** *scoops out the dripping contents of the watermelon and shares it with* **Sweetpeter**.

Father
Good. You'll learn on the job.
You're going to fight.

Sweetpeter (*disorientated*)
Where am I?

Father
In a long long war.

Sweetpeter
Who between?

Father
The government and the rebels.

Sweetpeter
I want to be a rebel.

Father
Good call.

Sweetpeter
Are you a rebel?

Father
Rebel commander.

Sweetpeter
You hate the government?

Father
I used to work for them but they went bust.
Then the rebels hired me.
War is my work.

Sweetpeter
You're a soldier?

Father
I'm a professional.
I kill who I'm paid to kill.

Sweetpeter
Why you not scared, mistah?

Father
I have a stone heart.

Sweetpeter
Do you have a wife, mistah?

Father
I lost her long time ago.

Sweetpeter
That's why you not scared.
No one miss you.

Sweetpeter *walks in front,* **Father** *behind, both faces in light frame.*

Father
Pick up the gun.
You are my shield.
Walk in front.
Stand up to lions.

Sweetpeter
I was a lion.

Father
That's right boy.

Sweetpeter
I had a mane and I had teeth and claws
I crunched up all kinds of men
I snapped off arms and legs
Like chicken bones
Everyone was afraid of me
And I was afraid of nothing.

Father
You stay in that zone, boy.

Sweetpeter
Where are we going?

Father
We're gonna kill everyone in Freetown.
Every living thing.
Keep moving.
Shoot anything in your way.

Sweetpeter and **Father** *sustain image of progress towards the capital.*

Scene Six

Mother *sits at her bar with a whisky. She is talking to the plaster cast of* **Gentlejesus***.*

Mother
The boy rebels.
They gouge and hack at living flesh,
They cut the living
Like a butcher
Cuts the carcass of a dead animal.
They feel nothing.

The blind old man,
The pregnant mother,

The naked toddler innocent of everything
Wandering lost across the street –
Out comes the machete and the axe;
The city is turning into hell.
The boy rebels feel nothing.

The rebels are coming,
Crowds of people are fleeing here from the country,
Thousands and thousands of people
Who have come through the bush barefoot and
Without food or weapons or money.
The whole country is pouring into the city.
Tomorrow we will wish that we could run into the sea
And swim across the ocean
Sooner than be trapped in hell.
The rebels are coming, the rebels are coming,
The only living things left will be vultures and dogs.
I am afraid that I will never see you again
My darling boy, my Sweetpeter.

Scene Seven

Father *and* **Sweetpeter** *take a roadside rest.*

Sweetpeter
What did you put on my head?

Father
Brown-brown.

Sweetpeter
What is it?

Father
It's medicine that gives you power
and makes you fear nobody.

Sweetpeter
It makes me feel tall
and other people look small.
Even you, Mistah Mistah.

Father
That's good medicine, boy.

Sweetpeter
Give me more.

Father
Stand up.

Father *cuts the boy's temple with a blade and applies a sticking plaster.*

Father
It gets there quicker that way.
How de body?

Sweetpeter
I feel strong,
I'll fight anyone.
I'll fight you, big man.

Father
You good boy.

Music: strong, aggressive.

Sweetpeter
I want kill.

Father
De boy's dream come true.

Sweetpeter
I want kill.

Father
You make good rebel soja boy,
You kill many bodies,
You kill beaucoup boy.

Sweetpeter (*leaping and straining to go*)
I want kill I want kill I want kill.

Movement sequence/dance to music. **Sweetpeter** *goes on the*
rampage killing every living thing. He shoots and he stabs and he hacks.
Father *follows, protected by* **Sweetpeter**.

Father
You like killing?

Sweetpeter
Show me a better job.

Father
Who will you kill when every living thing is dead, boy?

Sweetpeter
I'll kill you.

Father
You'll kill me?
You can't kill me.

Sweetpeter
Why not?

Father
I'm already dead, boy.

Sweetpeter
That's cool.
I want to be like you.
When you kill you don't blink,
You don't even think about it when you do it.
You're cool.
That's the way I'm gonna be.

Father
I've been fighting way too long.
You don't wanna be like me.

Sweetpeter
Don't tell me I can't be what I wanna be.
I've heard that before.
I can be anything I want to be.

Father
So who you gonna kill
When there's no one left but me?
When this war's over
I'll take my wages and move on.

Sweetpeter
To another war?

Father
Yeah.
Another and another and another.

Sweetpeter
I'll come with you.
I'm good aren't I?

Father
You're good,
Too good to be a slave.

Sweetpeter
What do you mean, slave?
You got the power, mistah.
You're no slave.

Father
There's different types of slave, boy.
I was a slave in a ship,
But you don't get that no more.
I was a farm slave
But they've gone too.
Now there's war slaves.
The worst slave you can be
Is a war slave.
You know why?

Sweetpeter
No.

Father
You just kill other slaves.

Sweetpeter *turns on* **Father**.

Sweetpeter
Why you comin' over this way all sudden, mistah?
You give me the gun, the brown-brown, the training.
You show me the light.
Now you want to take the light away,
Just like the preachers and the teachers
I have before you –
Every time I find my way
They say, 'That is enough, my boy,
You too advanced
You go too far!
Forget what we teach you,
Forget all we promise –
Back into the bush with you,
Back into the bush!'
Un-learn, un-read, un-write.
Now you way too late, mistah!
Don't un-train me –
I won't un-fight!

Father
Alright boy.
You go your way,
I'll go mine.

Father *sees someone and instantly pulls* **Sweetpeter** *to floor.*

Sweetpeter
Who's that, mistah?

Father
Get down! Down!
The big boys have come.
There's your chance.

They crouch on the floor and watch **Gentleknight**, *a Red Beret.*

Sweetpeter
Who are they, mistah?

Father
That's the British army, boy.

Sweetpeter
Here? The British army?

Father
That's the Red Berets.
Best trained best armed soldiers in the world, boy.
You keep out of sight.

Sweetpeter
I'm not afraid.

Father
You should be, boy.

Scene Eight

Gentleknight *the paratrooper is talking to audience as if they were his platoon. He is accompanied by a Government soldier.*

Gentleknight   First objective is to secure both the airport and the harbour, second is to get all of the European nationals out of the country, third is to stop the massacre on the streets.
The rebels have killed five thousand in six days.
Make no mistake, without intervention, the rebels will take the capital.
You need to know the difference between the rebel army and government troops. Not as easy as you might think.

The rebels prefer AK 47s; they're diamond-funded. They dress like rap-stars – they're usually stoned on cocaine, dope, sometimes heroin, and also drunk; the plasters on their face cover razor cuts in which they blend gunpowder and cocaine.

The government troops are British-funded, so they have old SLRs. They're more laid-back – that is, they're stoned, but mostly on dope. They hate the rebels, they like the English.

The rebels are often very young, I mean ten, eleven, twelve years old. Don't mess with them and get over qualms you might have about shooting at kids – they'll shoot you dead on sight.

But remember, we shoot only in defence.

Scene Nine

Mother *sees* **Sweetpeter** *approaching. He looks very different from when she saw him last. Neither* **Father** *nor* **Mother** *recognise each other.*

Mother
Sweetpeter?!

Father
How does she know your name, boy?

Sweetpeter
She's my mother, mistah.

Father
You said your mother was dead.

Sweetpeter
I lied to you.
Don't worry, mistah,
I kill her now.

He turns his gun on **Mother**.

Father (*looking closely at* **Mother**)
Don't do that, boy.

Sweetpeter
Why not?

Father
Put it down, boy.

Sweetpeter
Every living thing, right?

Father
Not now. Not her.

Sweetpeter
You're weak, big man.
I can do it.
Watch me.

Father
Put it down.
That's an order

Sweetpeter
'Kill your parents' –
That was an order.

Father
Drop it.

Sweetpeter (*turns the gun on* **Father**).
Stay away.

Father
Put it down.

Sweetpeter
I'll kill you, mistah.

Father
Give it me.

Sweetpeter *shoots* **Father** *three times.* **Father** *advances through the fire and takes the gun from* **Sweetpeter**. *He takes out a heavy knife from a sheath at his belt. He chops* **Sweetpeter** *at the wrist.* **Sweetpeter** *howls in pain and exits.* **Mother** *and* **Father** *look at each other.* **Father** *goes to leave without speaking.*

Mother
What is your name?

Father
I have no name.

Mother
Roll up your sleeve.

Father *rolls up sleeve to reveal a letter V branded on his arm.*

Mother
'V' for '*Victory*', 'His Majesty's Ship *Victory*'.

Father
And you?
What is your name?

Mother
I have no name.

Father
Show me your arm.

She pulls aside her dress to reveal the same letter to him.

'V' for '*Victory*'
'His Majesty's Ship *Victory*'.
It's you.

Music / dance between the **Father** *and* **Mother**.

Mother
Find our son.

Father
I will.

Father *exits.* **Mother** *calls after him.*

Mother
Don't seek a boy without a hand.
Look amongst the wildlife,
The rats and the dogs and the crows.

Scene Ten

Sweetpeter (*rap reprise – one-handed*)
I've been a fish a boy a bird

A boy a bat a boy a bird
I was lion
I was manboy
Now I'm dog
Three-legged street dog
With sores on my back
No teeth to pick at carcass
Or corpse
I'm near-to-dead dog
Near-to-dead

You lose a life you find a life you lose another
You find a life you lose a life you find another
I was born with seven lives
And I've used six
Next time I lose a life
I won't get another
There'll be no one left
To love my mother.

Gentleknight *is driving along in his armoured car with* **African soldier**. *He swerves to avoid* **Sweetpeter**.

African soldier
Bloody dog!

Gentleknight (*gets out*)
It's not a dog,
It's a lad.
He's been cut.

African soldier (*gets out*)
Get back inside!

Gentleknight
He's been amputated.
Get him in the car.

African soldier
He's a rebel.
Leave him.

Gentleknight
He's a child.

African soldier
They're the worst.
Don't you know that?

Gentleknight
Of course I do.
He'll live if we're quick.

Drumbeats/shots.

Get him in.
I don't want an RPG up the arse.

Sweetpeter *joins very rough ride to percussion and drum. He is in great pain.*

Scene Eleven

Father (*distressed, to anyone who will listen*)
Have you seen a dog without a paw?
Have you seen a bird without a wing?
Have you seen a rat without a tail?
No?
Then have you seen my son?
He has a name.
His name is 'Sweetpeter'.
Have you seen him?
Do you know him?

Scene Twelve

Gentleknight *is attending to* **Sweetpeter**. **Sweetpeter**
speaks very quietly.

Sweetpeter
Where am I? Where am I?

Gentleknight
I'll tell you where you are.
You are in the infirmary of a British warship,
HMS *Victory*.

You are safe here.
We'll look after you.
You are going to be alright.
When the ship docks in England,
They will take you to a military hospital in London.

Sweetpeter
You saved my life sir.

Gentleknight
I almost killed you, young man.
You've been concussed a long time.

Sweetpeter
You saved my life.
I was a dog,
A dirty stinking dog.

Father *enters*.

Father
Have you seen a boy without a hand?

Gentleknight
Thousands of them.
What's special about him?

Father
He's my son.

Gentleknight
Does he have a name?

Father
Sweetpeter.

Gentleknight
I might know him,
But I can't tell you anything.

You will have to prove that you're his father.
Sorry.

Father
I have no proof.

Father *stands useless.*

Gentleknight
I'm telling you nothing.
Someone cut his hand off.
You might mean him harm.
Can you bring his mother?

Father *nods his head.*

Father
I'll ask her if she'll come.

Father *turns to go.*

Gentleknight
She will need to bring proof too.

Father
Thank you sir.
I'll be back.

Gentleknight
A holiday picture or a school photo,
Something like that.

Father
Yes sir.

Gentleknight
With the mother.
Together, right?

Father
Yes sir.

He exits.

Scene Thirteen

Music/narrative through images. **Sweetpeter** *travels to London.*
Father *goes to* **Mother**. **Mother** *takes picture of* **Sweetpeter**
from the wall. They go together to **Gentleknight**.

Gentleknight
I am sorry to tell you
HMS *Victory* sailed for England at dawn.

Silence.

Father (*to* **Mother**)
We've lost him.
He's gone for ever.

Mother
We will hear from him.
He always comes back.

Father
I will find him.
However long it takes.
I will find him.

Whole company dance: 'War' (Bob Marley)

Scene Fourteen

Scene changes to place at start of the play – to London. The **Father**
*is a beggar in the city. He sits on a bucket and shows everyone a picture
wrapped in polythene on a stick. 'SWEETPETER, MY SON' is
written crudely above it. He begs for money.*

Father
Tonight is the coldest night of all.
To put it bluntly
I am feeling so hungry,
So desperately hungry,
That when I sit down outside
In the open cold

I feel empty but full of fear.
It is very early in the morning.
There's nobody around.
I am so hungry that I feel the cold air
Blowing through me.
Every part of me is shivering.
Yet I dare not move.

What if Sweetpeter walked past while I was away?
That is my fear.

I long for my son –
Why has not one person seen me here
In the middle of the city?
One person who knows my boy
And tells him of myself, his father,
Who holds his image aloft
That all the world can see him,
That all can love him like I do?

Where are you, my boy,
Where are you?
Sweetpeter
Sweetpeter
Sweetpeter.

His head drops and he sleeps.

Scene Fifteen

Music. **Sweetpeter** *enters and silently observes his* **Father**. *He is now a modern college boy in South London. Where his hand was he has a prosthetic glove. During the following, the scene reverts to the* **Mother'***s home and the London setting evaporates.* **Sweetpeter**, *in the course of the entire following speech, physically brings his parents together.*

Sweetpeter
Hello Mother,

I am so sorry that I have not been in touch with you for so
      long –
For two years and eleven months and five days.
I have been a coward.
And I'm sorry, Mother.

I'm so sorry.
They brought me to England and they mended my arm
And offered me a passage home,
To you, to Sierra Leone.
I said 'no' and I claimed asylum here in England.
To be safe, I changed my name –
That's why it took so long for Father to find me.

I found him, Mother,
Begging in the street
With a picture of me on a placard.
My father, the commander, the mercenary,
The hollow man.
So different now, Mother,
I went back to look at him many times.
He could not see me.
I watched him in rain and in snow.
I saw him shiver and shake.

Britain gave me asylum because I was a victim of war.
People have been kind to me.
They do not know that I was a murderer
And that I tried to shoot you,
My own mother.

I'm at college and I'm well, Mother.
I'm studying video and film at a college in Deptford,
Which is in the south of London.
My magic did not last the journey.
I'm twenty-one and I'll be twenty-two
Just like anyone else,
And I don't want ever to be
Anything or anyone else but me.

What I want to say,

What I want to ask is
Can I come home?
My vacation begins next month
And I have the money to come and visit you.

The parents are now within touching distance and they at last embrace.
Sweetpeter *now embraces his* **Father**. *Observed by his* **Father**,
Sweetpeter *now embraces his* **Mother**. *The family are united.*
Music: 'How Long?' (King Masco).

The Playground

Kay Adshead

About the Author

Kay Adshead was born in Manchester and now lives and works in London. She is an actor/playwright/poet, trained at RADA and an extensive acting career includes playing Cathy in the BBC drama series *Wuthering Heights*, and Linda in Mike Leigh's film *Kiss of Death*. She has written over fifteen theatre plays, including *Thatcher's Women*, *Juicy Bits*, *The Bogus Woman*, *Animal*, *Bites*, and *Bones*. She is Artistic Director of award-winning theatre company Mama Quillo (theatre for change) and *The Playground* was its first production.

About the Play

I wrote *The Playground* for my daughter Raphael's school, where it was performed in 1998, as part of their centenary celebrations. Hotham is, and was, a lovely school, but the building is grim Victorian and the playground, despite best efforts, was bare and forbidding. I dedicate the play in 2008 to Dylan Adshead, who has just started school.

One option is that *The Playground* can be performed with a minimum of between fifteen and twenty children. This involves a two-tier cast – the principals Ola, and the Spirits (School, Playground, Copper Beech), and the company, who divide all the other parts between them including the narrative line. Or conversely, the narration can be taken by just one child or by one or two, etc.

Equally, the play can also be acted by a class of children, thirty or so, doubling some roles. Most exciting and challenging (and it exists like this in this version) would be if the entire school were to mount the project.

The Playground is intended as an epic and democratic spectacle inspired by the magic of West Africa. Children who don't want to act can sing or make music (inventing and making their own instruments), show their paintings or impersonate animals, or be ghosts, or show off their playground skills. All children should have their chance to shine.

In this (wildly ambitious) text version the narrative chorus is huge and it is possible that every single junior has a speaking role. The challenge of creating a seamless narrative line out of so many individuals should be tackled very creatively like a game, and the play should flow scene into scene without scene changes.

Similarly, costume changes should be simple and 'rough' in feel with the children's own artwork at the heart of the play and integral to the spectacle.

The three Spirits all wear full body masks (very common in African ceremonies) and the creation of each one could be a class project. The play should be acted in a square or circle with audience on all sides. It would be best acted in the playground – in the dark with floodlights would be exciting, though the children would need microphones or to speak loudly. But it could also be acted in the school hall. The people (mums, dads, friends) who come to see this play could pay something (whatever they can) and the money used to make lots and lots of playgrounds more beautiful places.

Characters

Ola

Spirit of the Playground
Spirit of the Great Copper Beech
Spirit of the School

Children, *who play in the playground now – and who narrate the play*

Ghosts of the Past
Ghost of Queen Mary
Ghost of Queen Mary's Daughter

Teacher 1, **Teacher 2**

Mum 1, **Mum 2**, **Mum 3**, **Mum 4**

School Nurse
Smiling Teacher

Governor 1, **Governor 2**, **Governor 3**, **Governor 4**, **Governor 5**, **Governor 6**

Crabby Old Man
Nice Old Lady 1
Even Nicer Old Lady 2
Demolition Man
Garden Centre Owner
Timber Merchant
Paint Shop Man
Workman 1, **Workman 2**, **Workman 3**

Scene One

The Playground – playtime – **Children** *– shouting, screaming, running, jumping.*

Gradually, we make out a little girl, about ten or eleven; music – African pipes – very strange and far away; she weaves in and out of the other children.

The children's games accelerate unnaturally; the African pipes become stranger and more insistent. In the middle of the furious and raging playground the little girl stands still, her eyes full of tears, her lips trembling. Suddenly, she lifts her eyes to the sky and, with clenched fists, lets out an ear-shattering scream!

All the children stop playing and stare at the little girl. A teacher with a whistle stares in amazement. Everyone freezes. Absolute silence.

Child Narrator 1   And the school said

Sceptical Child   The school said? . . . The *school* said?

Child Narrator 1 (*firmly*)   And the school said

Spirit of the School   What's the matter with her?

Spirit of the Copper Beech   She's very sad

Child Narrator 2   – Said the Great Copper Beech – that had been growing in the playground for hundreds of years

School   Why?

Copper Beech   She comes from another country, a beautiful place where there's lots of trees and plants and flowers and insects and fish . . . and even animals

Child Narrator 3   And the playground

Child Narrator 4   Who also had a voice

Child Narrator 5   Though a very small one – said

Spirit of the Playground   But why does she scream?

Copper Beech   Because you're so ugly

School   Steady on

Playground (*lump in throat*)   Ugly?

Copper Beech   Yes, ugly – she thinks you're the ugliest place on Earth

Child Narrator 6   The Playground

Child Narrator 7   – Like the little girl –

Child Narrator 8   Was very sad to hear this

Child Narrator 9   Because he knew it was true.

Scene Two

The sad little girl from Scene One is sitting on a chair. All around her are **Teachers**, **Governors** *and a* **School Nurse**. *The older Year 5 and 6 children play these parts, but they must wear big built-up shoes, almost like stilts and they must all have 'hairdo hats' (male and female) – same as when they play mums and dads; this shows they are grown-ups.*

Very fast.

Teacher 1   It was the heat

School Nurse   It was the cold

Teacher 2   Delirium

School Nurse   Irascibility

Teacher 3   Bought on by

School Nurse *and* **Teacher** *together*   Global warming! Unsuitable footwear!

All   Isn't that right dear?

They all look at **Ola** *who stares back terrified.*

All   Isn't that right? (*Leaning in closer.*)

School Nurse   We won't know

Teacher   What's wrong

School Nurse   Unless you tell us

All (*leaning in more*)   Will we?

Ola *leans back.*

School Nurse (*not unkindly*)   Lost your tongue

Ola *claps hand over her mouth.*

Scene Three

Ola *and the* **Spirit of the Playground**.

Ola   I'm sorry

Playground   It's alright

Ola   I hope I haven't offended you

Playground (*gloomily*)   No – not at all

Pause.

Ola   I have
I'm sorry
I've hurt your feelings

Playground   No . . . No . . . Not at all

Ola (*quickly*)   You don't have any trees or flowers

Playground   That's right

Ola   There's no soft grass to sit on, or cool earth, or
running water

Playground   No

Ola   Nowhere to safely climb

Playground   Oh, there's been accidents, horrid they were

Ola   You're all cracked and crumbly

Playground   I know

Ola   On cold days you're hard, and when I fall I graze myself

Playground   Oh, I hate the cold weather

Ola   And on hot days you steam and stink

Playground   I know! I know! It's embarrassing. I've been told, it's a problem

Ola   I've looked and looked for birds

Playground   They're there – high overhead. You need good eyes. They don't land here

Ola   And there's nothing to do

Playground   Apart from chase each other, get tired, and cross, and be silly

Ola   So you see I hope you don't think I'm unkind

Pause.

Playground   I was 'nice' once
I remember . . . children liked me . . . people *visited* me, important people. Oh what a day, what an honour . . . Yes . . . I remember

Child Narrator 10   And the old, sad, playground day-dreamed

Ghosts of Children Past *appear.*

Child Narrator 10   Of when he was young

They wear the clothes that would have been worn when the school was built in 1909.

Child Narrator 11   And happy

Child Narrator 12   When the children, thrilled with the brand new school

Child Narrator 13   Thought the Playground

Child Narrator 14   Was indeed beautiful

The **Ghost Children** *all start to play, but games of 'the old days'. Skipping, the children chant 'Salt, Mustard, Vinegar, Pepper'; other children play 'Dabs' or '5 Stones', or 'Conkers'.*

Ola *walks among them. She is amazed by the* **Ghost Children**, *in their strange clothes, and their funny games. For the first time, she laughs and tries to join in with them.*

African drums, impressive and urgent. Suddenly a grand figure appears, this is the **Ghost of Queen Mary**, *and her* **Daughter**; *the* **Ghost Children** *stop playing and start to cheer wildly, waving little Union Jacks.* **Ola** *joins them; the drumming is even louder and grander.*

Ola   Who's that?

Ghost Child 1   What?

Ola   Who's the lady in the big hat?

Ghost Child 2   Are you having us on?

Ola   No

Ghost Child 2   Did you hear that? She says, 'Who's that?'

All the children laugh.

Ghost of Queen Mary (*swathed in furs, she speaks just like a queen*)   I am here today, with my dear daughter

Daughter *smirks prettily.*

Ghost of Queen Mary   To visit this beautiful modern and three-tiered school

School   Ooh I was modern then, I was that modern, *trendy* I was really

Ghost of Queen   With its magnificent and spacious playing area

Playground (*proudly*)   I was beautiful that day; they hung coloured flags, red, white and blue on my railings and shiny red ribbons on my gate, and on my steps they put big pots of . . . of . . .

Queen Mary   With its many plants

Copper Beech   Geraniums

Playground   Thank you. That was it

Queen Mary   Trees and shrubs of inherent beauty

Copper Beech   Many? I don't remember many. I've always been the most beautiful tree hereabouts

School   No . . . There were others: an apple tree, an oak

Queen Mary   Making it a truly splendid place for our children, and our children's children, to learn and grow

Polite applause.

Ola   But you still haven't told me who she is

Playground   You mean you really don't know?

Ola   No

Playground   That's the Queen of England

Ola   Is it?

All Spirits   Yes

Ola   The Queen! The real Queen of all England! I must talk to her. Queen! Oh Your Majesty! Can I speak to you? Can I? The playground isn't beautiful any more. It's old and sad and . . . and . . .

As ghosts, **Queen Mary** *and her* **Daughter** *and the* **Ghost Children** *in the playground start very slowly to move away from the calling* **Ola**, *as if a disappearing dream.*

Ola (*more desperate*)   Oh don't go, please. You can help, you're an important person, rich, I'm sure you're a nice woman. You've got kind eyes. Even if you have got a funny voice. And a fur coat

The **Ghost Children**, *the* **Queen** *and her* **Daughter** *have vanished.*

Ola   With all your money, couldn't we make the playground nice?

Ola *is alone with* **School**, **Playground**, *and* **Copper Beech**. *She's very despondent.*

School (*feebly*)   Cheer up!

Scene Four

Classroom. Children sitting on the carpet. **Ola** *stands; beside her is her* **Smiling Teacher**.

Ola   I come from a small village, Oko, just outside the Okomu Forest Reserve which is west of Benin City in a country called Nigeria in West Africa. My school is three miles away and has children from three other small villages round about. Every day I walk to school

Child 1   On your own?

Ola   No, with my five brothers and sisters and the other seventeen children from my village. If we are very late, we take the straight dirt road from Oko to Okomu. But mostly we zigzag across the fields into the forest reserve. We see forest elephants, white-faced monkeys, chimpanzees, giant forest hogs and lizards and maybe even a leopard

The children are wide-eyed.

There are of course many, many trees, some are fruit trees, mango, guava, pineapple and sometimes we will stop and climb or shake down an orange or a lime. We pass by a small stream full of fish which we might try to catch in our hand as we paddle across

Child 2 (*appreciatively*)   Cool!

Ola   Yes the water is very cool

The class laugh, but not unkindly.

Smiling Teacher   Go on Ola

Ola   The sky is very blue, and big, much bigger than your English sky

Child 3 (*sarcastic, under breath*)   I bet

Ola   And the sun is very hot, I think that too must be bigger

Child 3   It would be

Ola   And more yellowy, and all the plants and flowers and trees are more beautiful

Child 3 (*under breath*)   And much bigger

Ola (*delighted*)   Yes, how did *you* know?

Scene Five

Monday morning in the Community Room. **Parents** *and* **Teachers** (*in their stilt shoes and hairdo hats*). *They sit around drinking tea and chomping cakes. They face a window that looks out on to the playground.*

Mum 1   She's got a point

Mum 2   Mmm?

Mum 1   The new girl, look at it

Teacher   Oh yes absolutely

Pause as they sip tea.

Mum 1   What do you mean?

Teacher (*absent-minded*)   Sorry?

Mum 1   What did you say? I thought I heard you say 'Absolutely'. What did you mean by that?

Teacher   The playground, it's ever so ugly. Has been for as long as I can remember

Dad 1 (*finishing one cake, picking a big cream bun off a plate*)   As long as that?

Teacher   Yes

Long pause.

Mum 1 (*slams down cup on plate*)   Do you think we could just listen to ourselves for a moment here?

Dad 1 (*mouth crammed with cake*)   What?

Mum 1   That playground, it's . . . it's a monstrosity, it's huge and drab, and there's nothing to do out there

Mum 2   Nothing

Mum 3   The children swing from the rafters under the shed

Mum 4   It's dangerous, won't be long before there's an accident

Dad 1 (*still eating*)   It's unwelcoming

Mum 1   *Very* unwelcoming

Mum 2   Especially to new mums

Mum 4   And it's frightening

Teacher   Frightening?

Mum 4   Yes, if you're six or seven, or even eleven, it can be a frightening place

Teacher   No, I think you've gone a bit far there. I mean it's no Kew Gardens but it's not a House of Horror

Mum 1   And why isn't it, tell me

Teacher (*puzzled*)   Why isn't it a House of . . . ?

Mum 1   No . . . Why aren't there any flowers or plants or insects or trees; and why isn't there anything for the children to do out there. It's just tarmac, square after square. It's . . . it's a disgrace; that's what it is and it's about time we did something

Dad 1 (*mouth still full of cake*)   Absolutely . . . instead of stuffing our faces every Monday

Scene Six

Ola *is standing in the centre. Around her are* **Playground**, **Copper Beech** *and* **School**. *They are all whispering to her – secrets. On tape, we hear snatches of these. They sound exciting.* **Ola** *is wide-eyed and delighted. Through this we also hear the* **Narrators**.

Child Narrator 15   And the Playground, the School and the Copper Beech

Child Narrator 16   Their spirits

Child Narrator 17   Because places have spirits, just like people and animals

Child Narrator 18   So do things

Child Narrator 19   The stones under our feet

Child Narrator 18   A leaf

Child Narrator 19   Even a cockroach. If you hadn't already gathered

Child Narrator 20   The spirits told Ola their stories

Child Narrator 21   The stories of their lives

Child Narrator 22   And in these stories were many secrets

Child Narrator 23   Exciting secrets. Many about their ancestors

Child Narrator 24   The spirit of the school told of the searchlights fixed on the great iron gates to look for Zeppelins during the Great War

Child Narrator 25   And how the children knitted socks and gloves for soldiers to be sent out to the trenches

Child Narrator 26   Which were terrible places

Child Narrator 27   And the spirit of the Great Copper Beech told how when the Second World War ended

Child Narrator 28   On 8 June 1946, a notice from the king was pinned on her trunk and the notice said . . .

On tape we hear . . . 'I send this personal message to you and all other boys and girls . . . For you have shared in the hardships and dangers . . .'

Child Narrator 29   And the playground who told many surprising things

Child Narrator 30   Told Ola something that made her very excited

Everything stops.

Ola   A secret garden? What on earth do you mean?

Scene Seven

All the **Children** *now stand holding branches. They make a shifting forest.* **Parents** *and* **Teachers** *weave in and out. It is very tangled and overgrown but they are enchanted.*

Mum 1   My goodness

Mum 2   Take care

Mum 3   I didn't think this was school land

Dad 1   Tucked away here all these years

Mum 3   Well it's too overgrown for the children to play in now

Mum 2   There's lots of wild plants here, I wouldn't be a bit surprised if there's one or two rare ones

Mum 3   And look at all these butterflies, I've never seen so many

Children *appear, holding butterflies, bees, dragonflies on sticks, fluttering in the tangle.*

Mum 1   Well it's certainly got potential

Mum 4   Of course you couldn't have too many children here at one time

Dad 1   It's like a jungle. And what's this?

Ola *stands ahead of them – she's smiling.*

Ola   It's an open-air classroom. Isn't it absolutely lovely?

Child Narrator 31   Ola loved the open-air classroom

Child Narrator 32   Which was built on a wooden platform

Child Narrator 33   With a rickety wooden roof

Child Narrator 34   And was open to the sun and the wind and the rain

Child Narrator 35   And was half buried in dandelions

Child Narrator 36   And dog daisies and hollyhocks, and delphiniums

Child Narrator 37   Foxglove, iris, white and purple

Child Narrator 38   And four different types of clover, one type never before seen in London

Child Narrator 39   And even wild rhubarb

Child Narrator 40   Ola loved the classroom. Because it was a little bit like her school

Child Narrator 41   Back home in her village, Oko

Ola (*to teachers and parents, very politely*)   Could I have my lessons out here please?

Scene Eight

Governor 1   Absolutely not!

Public meeting at school. A platform of **Councillors** *and* **Governors**, *'important' people who decide how you spend money. Played by older children in built-up shoes but unlike Parents and Teachers they are all in dark suits (male and female variety). The audience now become the body of the public meeting, the actors sitting or standing among them.*

Governor 2   Nobody's saying that

Governor 3   It's just a matter of priorities

Governor 4   Managing resources

Governor 5(*kindly*)   Which are not infinite

Governor 6   As everyone knows

Governor 1   The school spending budget is stretched as it is

Governor 2   New hot water boiler for the Kitchens

Governor 3   Repainting the Lower Hall

Governor 4   Reslating

Governor 5   Pipe lagging

Governor 6   Yes . . . (*Surprised.*) pipe lagging?

Governor 1   There's a whole list of essentials

Governor 2   Absolute essentials

Governor 3   That bleed the school dry before you start thinking about (*He starts to guffaw.*) renovating some beaten-up . . .

Governor 4   Falling-down

Governor 5   Woodwormy old

Governor 6   Totally impractical

Governor 1   Given our climate

Governor 2   Bit of a shed

Governor 3   That goes under the name of 'open air classroom'.

Pause.

Mum 1 (*standing up from the audience*)   So that's your final word, is it?

Governor 2   Yes

Governor 2   Yes

Governor 3   Yes

Governors 4–6   Yes!

Mum 1   Right then, we'll just have to raise the money ourselves won't we?

Ola   May I suggest that to effect an immediate economy the gentleman stops smoking his pipe.

Child   And here's 50p!

Cheers.

Scene Nine

Child Narrator 42   So the mums and dads and teachers and children of the school

Child Narrator 43   Started a campaign

Child Narrator 44   To raise money

Child Narrator 45   To mend the open-air classroom

Child Narrator 46   In the secret garden

Child Narrator 47   And to make the poor, old, sad

Child Narrator 48   And ugly playground

All   Beautiful

Scene Ten

Garden. The **Children** *of now (the* **Narrators***) holding twigs and branches. The same strange African pipe music we heard at the beginning only even softer.*

Ola (*whispering*)   What's the matter, secret garden?
Why won't you speak to me?

She waits.

I know you have a lovely voice
A lovely voice, as soft and light as a cloud

The music is sad.

Playground speaks to me

Spirit of the Playground *appears.*

Ola   And School

Spirit of the School *appears.*

Ola   And the Great Copper Beech

Spirit of the Tree *appears.*

Ola   Why won't you?

Playground   She's shy. Aren't you, secret garden?

Copper Beech   No one's been around here for years

School   Years and years

Copper Beach   Probably hasn't got much to say anyway, left to herself all these years

Playground   She's been very neglected

Copper Beech   Overgrown

School   A bit of a jungle

Pause.

Ola (*whispering*)   You're wrong. The secret garden is frightened

Playground   Frightened?

Ola   Yes, she is frightened, she is frightened of the men with axes

Scene Eleven

Ola *stands in the centre of the playground. The entire company, including* **Spirits**, *sit around her. They listen.*

Ola   I told you that I come from a country called Nigeria, from the rain forest, Okomu Forest, I told you of the many wonderful animals, the wild elephants, baboons, hippopotami, water bucks, of the strange birds, fish eagles, saddlebills, storks, kingfishers and vultures. And of the strange forest life, I told that I believe it is the most magical place on Earth, but what I did not tell you, is that it is one of the very few remaining areas of rain forest left in my country. For many years men with axes came to the forests, they chopped down all the great trees and took them on lorries to make into wood for the town or to send on ships to far-away countries; they cut back the plants and left the earth flat and bare and brown and in the rain the land turned to mud, and without any trees and plants in which to live in and eat, the animals ran away or started to slowly die, so the beautiful rain forests became empty wastelands, with no plants insects, birds, animals; as ugly and barren as poor old Playground here.

Dad 1   So what are you saying?

Mum 1   It's perfectly obvious what she's saying

Mum 2   To anyone with half a brain

Ola   Leave the secret garden alone please

Mum 2   I told you there's some rare wild flowers there, and the insect life is astonishing

Mum 4   All those butterflies, and there's a little pond at the end

Mum 2   I saw a bullfrog – a very unusual colour, and quite huge

Mum 3   Oh my goodness

Dad 1   But the children can't go in like that, it's a wilderness

Mum 3   Not with bullfrogs – my Darren hates frogs

Dad 1   We must make it nice

Mum 3   Yes, pull up all the weeds and plant a nice lawn, I say

Mum 4   Cut back the hedges

Teacher   A herbaceous border is always nice I think

Mum 3   Prune the trees back to a proper size

Mum 4   And get rid of that stagnant bit of pond

Ola   NO! NO! NO! NO! NO!

Pause, everybody astonished at **Ola***'s apparent fury.*

Teacher (*feebly*)   And what about the open-air classroom?

Child Narrator 49   The mums and dads

Child Narrator 50   And the teachers

Child Narrator 51   Surprised by Ola's fury

Child Narrator 52   And a bit embarrassed. After all she *was* a *new* girl

Child Narrator 53   Left the thorny issue of what to do with the secret garden

Child Narrator 54   For another day. And decided to try and raise money for the playground

Child Narrator 55   Though they had heard

Child Narrator 56   Most definitely

Child Narrator 57   And taken note of what Ola

Child Narrator 58   Had, so passionately, said

Scene Twelve

Mums *and* **Dads** *on a street corner in town.* **Mum 1** *is shaking a tin marked 'Playground Fund'.*

Mum 1   Please give generously. Invest in our children's future. Let's make the playground beautiful

A 'crabby' **Old Man** *with a stick approaches the* **Mum***, he is very cross.*

Old Man   Every time I come out, every flippin' morning there's one of you lot, 'research for this' . . . 'spare your flippin' change for that'. And what's this?

Mum *tries to speak; he looks at her can and interrupts.*

Old Man   Playgrounds! Ha! Now I've heard it all. We didn't have playgrounds. Played in the street we did, night after night (*Very aggressive, face pushed close to* **Mum**.)

Conkers! Never mind 'Ninja flamin' smurfin' rangers'. Marbles! Or seeing how far you could spit. Champ at that I was. Good for us . . . Character-building. (*He starts to leave.*)

Flippin' kids . . . Get it laid on with a trowel . . . Need a good . . .

Child Narrator 59   And the mums and dads

Child Narrator 60   As you can well believe

Child Narrator 61   After days of this, or similar

Child Narrator 62   Got quite discouraged

Child Narrator 63   Though of course there were many good

Child Narrator 64   And kind people

Old Lady 1 (*fumbling in purse*)   Dear, dear don't they have nice playgrounds

Old Lady 2   I thought they had to these days, you know . . . the EEC

Old Lady 1   I'm going to the EEC about my dentist. I've been to them before about my loose covers, lovely they were, the EEC tore Arding and Hobbs off a strip, here we are (*At last she puts in a shiny 5p! in the can.*)

Child Narrator 65   But mostly the shoppers

Child Narrator 66   Who were very busy, just ignored the mums and dads

A stampede of shoppers all with shopping bags floor the **Mums** *and* **Dads**.

Child Narrator 65   And the rattling tins

(**Mum 1** *is knocked down all skew-whiff.*)

Mum 1   Please give generously

Scene Thirteen

Meeting of **Parents** *and* **Teachers**.

Mum 1 (*counting out the money*)   Four pounds and twenty-six only

Dad 1 (*eating*)   Not bad

Mum 1   For one week! You want to stand out there all weathers

Mum 2   That's about enough for one geranium plant

Mum 3   Or two footballs

Mum 1   It's hopeless. (*Thoughtfully pacing.*) We've got to get organised

Mum 4   Come up with schemes

Mum 3   That's it

Mum 1   To make money . . . fast

Child Narrator 66   And so they all put their heads together

We see the **Parents** *and* **Teachers** *in a 'scrum'.*

Child Narrator 67   And came up with some smashing ideas

Mum 1 (*emerging from scrum*)   A sponsored walk!

Child Narrator 68   To raise money to make the playground beautiful

Back to scrum, more talk, around them we see sponsored walkers.

Teacher (*emerging from scrum*)   A sponsored read! For every book the children read they'll get a few pence towards the playground

The walkers turn into readers, one tries to walk and read and falls over.

Mum 3 (*from the scum*)   Cake sales! Every Friday the mums and dads will bake cakes and we'll sell them

A big cheer . . . a great rush to buy cakes. From the scrummage, **Parents** *and* **Teachers** *walk about inviting ideas from the audience on how to raise money to make the playground beautiful; there are lots of suggestions.*

Child Narrator 69   So this way, the mums and dads got lots of really wonderful ideas

Scene Fourteen

Ola *is alone with the* **Spirits of the Playground** *and the* **School** *and the* **Copper Beech**.

Ola (*whispering*)   Oh Playground, isn't it exciting

Playground   I'm dizzy with it all

School (*grumbling*)   Not sure about the car park scheme

Copper Beech   No, it'll be nice, weekends are lonely

Playground   Every Saturday and Sunday, I'm going to be a car park. A real proper car park. Imagine: people will pay a lot of money to park their cars all over me

Ola   And there's the car boot sales

Copper Beech   And the pet show

School   And the fancy-dress parade, and the tombola and the Friday ice-cream stall. So many clever and special things

Spirits *go*.

Child Narrator 70   And cleverest of all, the mums and dads and the teachers

Child Narrator 71   Had worked out a series of plans to approach

Child Narrator 72   Local businessmen

Child Narrator 73   Even a demolition company

Child Narrator 74   To donate materials

Child Narrator 75   And service

Child Narrator 76   To try and make the playground beautiful

Scene Fifteen

A crowd of **Mums** *and* **Dad**. *A gaggle of voices.*

Demolition Man   Hang on, hang on, you're telling me that for two weeks in summer I should donate a quarter of my workforce and half my machinery . . .

Garden Centre Owner   . . . All the left-over plants and trees and seeds and pots and potting compost

Timber Merchant   . . . All the offcuts . . .

Paint Shop Man   . . . All the discontinued lines, paint, and brushes and varnish

All Local Businessman   So that you can make a children's playground beautiful!

All Mums   That's right

All Businessmen   For free

All Mums   You heard! For free

All Businessmen   You're mad

Pause.

We'll do it

A huge cheer.

Child Narrator 77   But as the Playground became more and more sure

Child Narrator 78   Of becoming truly beautiful

Child Narrator 79   The secret garden, watching the timber merchant's man and the demolition men

Child Narrator 80   Became more and more frightened

Scene Sixteen

Ola *stands amid the children holding branches and the butterflies on sticks. African pipes closer and more urgent. The branches twitch nervously and the butterflies flutter.*

Ola (*whispering*)   Don't be afraid, secret garden (*The pipes seem to answer her.*)
I won't let the men with axes come
I won't let them chop down your trees
Or cut your long grasses
I won't let them fill in the pond (*The pipes speak to her.*)
I won't let them pull up your roots
I know you are magic
A magical place
I won't let them take it away

The **Spirits of the Playground** *and the* **Copper Beech** *and the* **School** *appear.*

School   What do you mean magic?

Copper Beech   It's never been magic before

School (*huffily*)   Why, she can't even speak like us

Playground   No, not in all these years

School   Not the least bit, teeniest bit magic

Ola   No. That's because she didn't have me

Scene Seventeen

Meeting: **Mums**, **Dads** *and* **Teachers**.

Mum 1   It's a miracle. We've done it. We've enough money, and manpower, and resources to completely dig up the tarmac playground, to resurface with a safe playing area, to build wooden climbing frames and swings and slides, to lay out deep wooden trenches and to plant many trees and shrubs and flowers. To create a rockery that children can play in, with little houses and a tree house. Oh, it will be a wonderful place

Mum 2   And what about the secret garden?

Mum 3   And the open-air classroom?

Mum 4   Yes, that needs attention

Mum 5   Tidying up

Dad 1   Clearing out

Mum 3   Hoeing

Mum 4   Replanting

Dad 1   Maybe we could have a big bonfire in there, all that garden refuse

Ola *appears in front of them. She is grim-faced and determined.*

Ola   If you disturb the secret garden, if you dig and cut and hoe and crop, you will destroy all the secret insect life, rare and special, all the tiny rare flowers and clovers and grasses. If you dig up the nettles, the butterflies, so many different colours will fly away and die. If you dredge up the little pond the frogs too will die, and the little fishes. Don't you know that secret places, places kept secret from people for years and years, keep their magic in the earth, in the air, in your English frost and dew. You will make it ordinary with your hoeing and trimming. Don't you realise. Don't you?

Everyone listens gravely.

Mum 1 (*quietly*)   Ola, tell everyone your idea. This is to celebrate the fundraising

Child Narrator 81   And Ola told everyone

Child Narrator 82   But in a quiet voice because she was still upset

Child Narrator 83   That in her country when something nice happens

Child Narrator 84   The whole village has a festival, a celebration with drumming, singing and dancing

Child Narrator 85   And feasting

Dad 1   It's a wonderful idea. We'll do it to celebrate our fundraising. The day before the bulldozers move in to make the playground beautiful

Child Narrator 85   Ola was happy, very happy for the playground

Child Narrator 86   Which was bare and ugly and had no plants or flowers or anything

Child Narrator 87   But she didn't know what they planned to do about the secret garden

Scene Eighteen

Ola *sits silently with the* **Spirits**.

Copper Beech   Are you nervous?

Playground   No, not a bit

Copper Beech   Won't the drills and the diggers and the bulldozers hurt?

Playground   No, don't you see, it's like I've been wearing this black treacly overcoat all these years and now I'm taking it off for the first time I'll feel the sun and wind and rain on my back

Copper Beech   Are you excited, School?

School   Very, I'm getting a lick of paint

Copper Beech   Well, I'm happy. It'll be nice to have new trees and plants and insects to talk to after all these years

Playground   But Ola, you're not happy

Scene Nineteen

Ola, *alone in the midst of the secret garden.* **Children** *with branches.*

Ola (*she whispers frantically*)   Oh, secret garden, I've spoken with an angry voice and tears in my heart, but I don't know if I was heard.

Was I?

Pan-pipes speak to **Ola**.

They won't come, will they? With their pruners and hoes. Will they? I know strong magic.

She stands, grandly, arms outstretched.

I call upon the spirit of the white-faced monkey.

Light change, a drumroll, occasionally a strange flutey pipe like the screech of a monkey.

And giant forest hog. (*Musical snorts.*) The fork-tongued lizard (*Musical flicking tongue.*) And the fiery leopard. (*Musical roar.*) I call upon the Spirit of the Forest to come to the secret garden, in London, England, which too is magic, even though it's English. I call strong magic. (*All the sounds together.*) To fight the men with axes. (*A cacophony.*)

On the one side of **Ola**, *very slowly as if from a dream, appear the* **Ghost Children**.

Ghost Child 1   They won't come.

Ola (*frantically calling up*)   Spirit of the white-faced monkey.

More musical screams, a lightning flash.

Ghost Child 2   Not here.

Ghost Child 3   This is England.

Ola   Spirit of the giant forest hog.

More musical snorts, a lightning flash.

Ghost Child 4   You'll be lucky.

Ola   And the leopard. (*Musical roar.*) And, and the lizard. (*Musical flicking tongue.*)

Ghost Child 5   I'm telling you they don't have no place here. They won't come.

Slowly, very slowly the music recedes.

Ola   What then?
What can I do?
Tell me? What strong magic can I use?
To stop the men with axes cutting away the secret garden?
I know
Of course
I know

Behind the **Ghost Children** *appears the* **Ghost of Queen Mary,** *and her strange* **Daughter.**

Ola   Yes, of course Your Majesty
Oh Great and Powerful Ancestor
(*The* **Daughter** *giggles.*) You can help

Queen Mary (*puzzled*)   Can I dear?

Ola   Of course

Queen Mary   What can I do?

Ola   Stop them cutting down the secret garden

Queen Mary   But, my dear, lawns have to be kept in trim
Privets cut back
Flower beds weeded and hoed
We simply can't let things just keep on growing

Ola   But what about the butterflies?

Queen Mary   What about them?

The **Daughter** *giggles.*

Ola (*exasperated*)   They will die, don't you see, or have their babies with nowhere to rest or feed, and they are so fragile and so beautiful.

Queen Mary   No no. They'll just flit somewhere else dear

Daughter (*in a high-pitched voice*)   They'll just flitty wit away
To other gardens
Making other gardens pretty witty

Ola   Are you sure? Are you?

Queen Mary (*hesitant*)   Yes . . . er, yes.
Anyway, my dear, is it really that important what becomes of a few measly butterflies? Is it?

Daughter   Measly weasly wutterflies and motts that bite!

Ola (*horrified and close to tears*)   Well what about the clover?

Queen Mary   Clover?

Daughter *giggles.*

Ola (*defiantly*)   Yes, four different types, very rare

Queen Mary (*sternly*)   Now aren't we getting the teensiest bit silly?

She starts to sneeze.

Daughter   Yes, silly willy it's only gwass

Ola   Well what about the bull frogs?

Daughter   Oh, howwid, froggie poggies

Queen Mary (*decidedly*)   And slimy

Daughter   And green. Aren't they froggies? Snakes are howwid too

Queen Mary   I never had much time for reptiles

Daughter   And crocodiles and crabs and lizards and, and

Queen Mary   Yes dear, so you see

Voice concern is touching.

Daughter   For the pogs and the wutters and – and (*She sneezes.*) and gwass

Queen Mary   But we mustn't make fusses

Daughter   About nothing

Queen Mary   Must we, dear?

The **Ghost Children** *melt away as do* **Queen Mary** *and her* **Daughter**. *The pan-pipes play very sweet and sad.*

Ola   I have failed you, secret garden. I'm sorry, I thought I had strong magic but I don't

Scene Twenty

The masquerade. Wild and wonderful. the whole playground is taken over by an African festival. A Nigerian celebration. Many of the masks are animals. The white-faced monkey, the forest hog, the lizard and the leopard.

Mum 1   Oh, this is wonderful, truly

Dad 1 (*eating*)   This African nosh is brilliant

Mum 1   You realise all of you this is the last time we'll be standing in the playground like this

Ola *appears.*

Mum 1   In the morning the men with the pneumatic drills will appear and the old playground will end up in slabs on the back of a ten-ton lorry

Mum 2   That's right. And we'll plant a new playground

Ola   Excuse me please?

Mum 1   Yes

Ola   Do you know what your plans are for the secret garden?

Mum 1 (*quietly*)   Yes Ola, we know

Scene Twenty-one

Very early morning, **Workmen** *arrive with their pneumatic drills into the now empty playground. We hear pan-pipes.*

Workman 1 (*looking about*)   They weren't kidding were they?

Workman 2   What's that then?

Workman 1   Look at it.

Workman 2   Ugly, you mean?

Workman 1 (*heaving his drill*)   If you ask me the sooner we start digging up this great black monstrosity the better.

Tape, the ferocious sounds of a pneumatic drill. Pan-pipes louder. Then drills. Then pan-pipes.

Child Narrator 87   So the workmen put the spoke of the drill into the ugly, black

Child Narrator 88   Treacly playground

Drums.

And a hole appeared

A cacophony of sound, made by the children and taped jungle music and the screeching cry of wild animals.

Child Narrator 89   And instantly, just like magic, a great crack zigzagged across the entire playground like a lightning flash

Ola   And from the steaming and fragrant crack sprang the tropical rain forest of Okomu, long grasses and trees and lush green vegetation

Child Narrator 90   And the other workmen. They too pressed their drills in to the old playground, and instantly more cracks sprang up, making a crazy pavement of the playground, and from these cracks sprouted pineapple trees and lime trees, orange trees and guava trees, with their glossy wet tongue leaves, and limes heavy as emeralds, orange trees like a thousand dimpled suns and best of all (sweet and juicy as a damp shower) the guava

During all this, the acting area is transformed by the children's paintings and models of the magical rain forest.

Child Narrator 91   And soon there were so many cracks in the playground made by the men with drills that it was covered in a lush and undulating, perfumed forest of trees and plant and flowers and insects and birds and all the animals

Ola   And high up in the trees swung the white-faced monkey

Child in monkey mask appears, musical monkey noises.

And forest elephants roamed freely

Children as forest elephants, musical elephant music.

And the giant water hog

Children appear as hogs, musical hog.

And the lizard
And the leopard

More music. And now the whole playground is a magical tropical forest. The **Workmen** *look about flabbergasted.*

Workman 1   S'truth

Workman 2   Strike a light

Workman 3   Well I'm a monkey's uncle

Workman 1 (*monkey approaches*)   I think I need a Nescaf . . . Ahhhhhhhhh

Child Narrator 92   For the mums and dads and teachers and governors who turned out to be not so bad after all

Child Narrator 93   Had decided to touch not a blade of grass, in the secret garden, not a clover leaf, not a butterfly wing, not a dandelion, a daisy, not a single stone

Child Narrator 94   But to keep it exactly as it was. And Ola roamed, the new forest playground, playing tag with the chimps, with all the other children, riding on the back of the wild elephants, climbing the pineapple trees, swinging from the orange tree and lime and splashing in the purply green lagoon

Ola   I am very, very happy

Child Narrator 95   The tropical rain forest in our school is considered a very interesting phenomenon. Many important scientists, naturalists and students of the paranormal come to study it to this day. Thank you Mr Bellamy . . . Mr Attenborough

Two child impersonators in the audience stand, beam and nod.

Child Narrator 96   The money so arduously raised for the playground was used to look after the animals, but eventually the children had to keep on devising new schemes to raise money to feed the white-faced monkey, the water hog, the leopard and the lizard

Child Narrator 97   The water hog was particularly greedy

Scene Twenty-two

Outside shops.

Mum 1   Please give generously, feed the school leopard

Crabby Old Man *approaches*.

Old Man (*incredulous*)   Leopard, leopard, we didn't have no leopard, never saw a leopard (*He thinks.*), in fact I've never seen a leopard, well, unless you count that mangy one in Regent's Park

Mum 1   Oh, well, we've got a leopard, a paticularly beautiful one actually

Old Man   Have you?

Mum 1   Yes

Old Man   Can I see it?

Mum 1   Of course you can. Come on I'll take you

As they go off they pass the two **Old Ladies**.

Old Lady 1 (*to* **Mum**)   Very good idea. We've just been up there

Old Lady 2   Very novel. Just shows you what you can do with 5p

Scene Twenty-three

Ola *stands at the centre. Around her* **Spirit of the School**, **Spirit of the Playground**, **Spirit of the Great Copper Beech**. *In a greater circle, everyone, audience and actors.*

Spirit of the School   Thank you little girl. Before I saw only black brick and tar. Now everything is green and dappled and the sweet air hums.

Spirit of the Copper Beech   Thank you little girl. Before, no birds sang in my branches. Now the white monkey dances here. And what interesting conversations I shall have with the kingfishers and the eagles.

Spirit of the Playground   Thank you little girl. My back is green and soft and feels cool in the breeze. I am home to all the animals and insects, from the tiny scurrying ant to the mighty amber lion.

The pan-pipes are playing.

Ola (*turning around*)   And what of you, secret garden? Will you speak to me? Will you? Will you?

The pan-pipes get louder and louder. Gradually a small voice is coming through. It is the voice of a tiny child, soft and can only just be heard.

The Secret Garden (*whispers to* **Ola**)   Thank you!

The Odyssey

Hattie Naylor

About the Author

Hattie Naylor was born in London and was studying painting at the Slade School of Art when her first play *The Box* was accepted in the BBC Radio Young Playwrights Festival. Since then she has won several national and international awards for her radio plays. She has written for theatre, film, and opera and lives in Bristol. Recent radio plays include *Solaris*, and *Daphnis and Chloe*, theatre work includes *Mother Savage*, and *Alice Through the Looking Glass* for the Tobacco Factory.

About the Play

Kate Cross and Lee Lyford from Theatre Royal Bath came to me with the idea of adapting *The Odyssey*. I was determined to make it exciting, funny and relevant and a good introduction to classics for young people. It is our oldest 'action adventure' with monsters, gods, love and deceit. This I utilised without losing the layering in this rich tale that is the inspiration for so many stories across the world.

The Odyssey was first produced in 2002 by Theatre Royal Bath for 'Storm on the Lawn', an annual event in Bath in which sixty young people rehearse for three weeks leading up to five public performances, supported by a professional creative team, including a professional composer. It was directed by Lee Lyford and designed by George Naylor. The play particularly thrives on music between scenes and the use of sound for the sea and storms. There are extensive stage directions. I would advise an attempt to make the stage directions work before discarding them. I come from a visual art background and the stage directions in my scripts are as relevant as the text; often a percentage of the storytelling is done visually and the play can become unclear if they are not used. There was also extensive use of puppetry in the first production, a moat was used for the sea and several models of Odysseus's ship proved very useful in clearer storytelling. And just a small suggestion: we cast the smallest and most childlike of the young people to play the gods; this worked very well.

Characters

Laertes, *seventy, Odysseus's father*
Telemachus, *nineteen, Odysseus's son*
Penelope, *forty, wife to Odysseus, mother to Telemachus*
Suitors, *men of Ithaca (nobility), seeking Penelope's hand in marriage*
Antinous, *Achaean noble*
Eurymachus, *Achaean noble*
Hermes, *god – Zeus's messenger*
Zeus, *most powerful of the gods and leader*
Athene, *goddess of Wisdom*
Fates 1, 2 and **3**, *ancient triple goddesses who weave men's fates*
Hermes' Attendant
Calypso, *goddess (nymph)*
Nausicaa, *nineteen, princess of Phaeacia and daughter to King Alcinous*
Nausicaa's Maids
Odysseus, *forty*
Alcinous, *king of Phaeacia*
Demodocus, *Phaeacian storyteller*
Euryalus, *merchant trader at Alcinous's court*
Odysseus's Men 1, 2, 3, 4, 5 and **6**
Eurylochus, *loyal but weak servant to Odysseus*
Cyclops, *one-eyed monster, son of Poseidon*
Cyclops 1, 2, 3, 4, 5, *brothers to Cyclops*
Aeolus, *a king and Keeper of the Winds*
Circe, *goddess*
Circe's Attendants 1, 2, and **3**
Cerberus, *three-headed dog that guards Hades*
Charon, *the ferryman who takes the dead into Hades*
Teiresias, *Theban seer and prophet*
Anticleia, *Odysseus's mother*
Poseidon, *god of the Sea and brother of Zeus*
Melantho, *nineteen, malicious house-servant to Penelope*
Eurycleia, *faithful servant and nurse to Penelope*
Father 1, *father to Antinous*
Father 2, *father to Eurymachus*
Brother 1, *brother to Eurymachus*
Shades, *the dead wandering the halls of Hades*
Penelope's Women, *servants to Penelope*
Brothers, *brothers of those murdered by Odysseus*

Scene One

The great hall of Odysseus's palace. A state of tranquillity. Soundscape of sea and music. The peace is abruptly broken by a football rolling on to the stage – followed by the **Suitors**, *aggressively mimicking playing in a rowdy football match – they shout towards one another. Some are carrying cans of lager – filling the space with their disruption.*

Telemachus *and* **Laertes** *enter.*

Laertes, *old and frail, shouts above the noise and is ignored. The* **Suitors** *continue playing.*

Laertes   Cease. End. Stop. End this! . . . End this now!

Telemachus   End. End. Do as my grandfather bids.

Laertes   Stop this. Stop this now. Stop this all of you. This is a palace, the palace of Odysseus. Leave it, leave us here to await his return.

Penelope *enters, followed by* **Eurycleia**, *as* **Laertes** *speaks.*

Laertes   Leave us to await his return.

Penelope   End this! End this!

The **Suitors** *stop, all turn to listen to her. Silence.*

Penelope   You come about here drunk. Drinking and eating and wasting away all our livestock and wealth here – here in Odysseus's palace. When will you leave us?

Antinous   We will take our leave, Lady, when you have chosen one of us as a husband . . .

Telemachus   King Odysseus will return, my father is still alive and will return to see you all off.

Antinous   Odysseus has been gone for some twenty years since, what could prevent him from coming home, Telemachus? What could have kept your father away for so long?

Eurymachus   You must learn to accept his death, Lady, let grieving pass and choose another husband. Here are the finest, the best, the most noble men of Ithaca, all of whom are here waiting for your choice.

Antinous   Free us by choosing one of us. Choose one and the others will be free to marry, once you have taken your pick. In not choosing you also deny happiness elsewhere, to the other women of Ithaca, awaiting husbands.

Laertes   When my son returns he will have plenty to say to you, Antinous, and your slanted words. Your head will be sliced into finest bacon and fried.

Suitor 1   He's been away for too long, old Laertes. He isn't coming home.

The **Suitors** *laugh.*

Penelope   I am weaving a great cloth. And every day I weave my sorrows away in threads of blue and green loss – shadows of the sea. When that work has finished, my weaving complete, my task over; when the length of my grief is woven into a thousand threads of that loss, then, I will consent to choose one of you. One of you – who is not even in the brightest corner – a shadow, a whisper of my golden man – my golden Odysseus – my true husband.

A football bounces. She turns to look and then exits.

Telemachus   Do you know no courtesy, no restraint? Can you not hear her words and entreaties to you? And you too, you over there that sit in silence and watch but say nothing, and eat and drink and play. You silent ones that let Antinous and Eurymachus do your talking for you. (*Birds – eagles – heard overhead.*) It is you, more, I believe, it's you more, that offend, that offend the gods.

Soundscape – eagles fight in air, squawking across the assembly.

Laertes   See, see there Telemachus, those fighting eagles.

The assembly look up.

He will return, see those eagles. He will return and devour all of you.

Eurymachus   No, old man. Two birds in the sky do not signify anything. The gods have abandoned you and your family, why else would they have kept Odysseus away from Ithaca, from his home, for so long. He has offended them in his battle lust, in his killing and is surely in Hades amongst the shades in death.

Laertes *and* **Telemachus** *exit.*

The **Suitors** *go back to their revelries and exit. Soundscaped knitting.*

Scene Two

Fate 1
Breathe breath my heart into knitting.
Knitting life lines.

Fate 2
The Way of the World.

Fate 3
The Wheel of fortune.

Fate 1
The Weather in the Streets.

Fates 2 *and* **3**
Pearl one, knit one, pearl one, knit one.

Possibly repeat.

Fate 1 *places a small island in the middle of the set and then adds the small figure of a man on the island.*

Fate 1
Some say we were bred at the beginning of time.
That time stood still before us,
That there was a moment,

An intake of breath before our birth – a moment of still,
Of silence of no, no nothing,
Before the knitting began.
Before the threading of life on to its mortal coil –
Before the threads of being were trapped
On to – life – matter.

Fate 2
Others say we are the word,
The doers, the seers and sayers
And there was nothing before us –
That everything could only be
When time began – when
The baby glistening eyes of us
Pierced into the bubble of the Universe.

Fate 3
And still others say we sprang from
The blood of Uranus
When Kronos cut him
And diminished him.

Fates 2 *and* **3**
Pearl one, knit one, pearl one, knit one.

Possibly repeat.

Fate 1
That our rivers of thread
Our rivers of being – our web –
Are life itself.
We are the curving dream
Round time.
We are the sisters three.
Pearl one, knit one, pearl one, knit one.

Possibly repeat.

Soundscaped knitting. The **Fates** *remain on stage, knitting, throughout the play.*

Scene Three

The Magic Shop (Olympus). **Hermes** *and* **Athene** *enters, he attempts to do a magic trick throughout the scene.* **Athene** *stands over the figure on the island with concern.* **Zeus** *enters and observes his daughter. Soundscape – of a man weeping in the far distance and the seashore.*

Zeus   How can you favour them?

Athene *turns to look at her father.*

Athene   Mhhm?

Zeus   How can you favour them?

Athene *looks back to the figure. Crying tapering off from soundscape.*

Zeus   Such fragile, decaying things, attached to places, names . . . each other, and their attachment to time, eating them up.

Athene   He is the best though, the very best amongst humanity.

Zeus   But he's sighing. His eyes are wet with tears. How can sighing be worthy?

Athene   He has been waiting for twenty years to return home. The more miserable of them would not be sighing – the more miserable of them would be blaming – blaming the gods, blaming us. Odysseus has more sense, more knowledge, more cunning. He is a fine specimen, a righteous way – he deserves our help. He deserves to be allowed home.

Zeus   Home?

Athene   Yes.

Hermes *manages to finally do his trick successfully – he claps himself.* **Athene** *and* **Zeus** *regard him with annoyance.* **Hermes** *continues with his magic tricks as soon as they return to their talk.*

Athene   The human heart needs a place to gather itself, to gather courage, civility, dignity – self. It is not a weakness. We know nothing of home – or the need for that place, for the universe is our house – every particle within it a part of us. But these humans, even one as resourceful as Odysseus, even he aches for this home – for Ithaca.

Zeus   He offended my brother.

Athene   He is dutiful to you. Poseidon is away, away from the Aegean, past the Nile, in those hot lands of the deserts. Make the goddess Calypso release Odysseus. Let him go home.

Zeus   Your favourite, this man?

Athene   An exceptional man. Surely the best, the best they can be should be rewarded, celebrated, favoured. Cloud Gatherer, Holder of Thunder, Kronos's son, let him go home.

Zeus *pauses, considering.* **Hermes** *completes another trick.* **Zeus** *looks towards the figure on the island and finally speaks.*

Zeus (*to* **Hermes**)   Go tell Calypso to release Odysseus.

Hermes *jumps down from the table, stuffing magic tricks in his pockets.*

Zeus (*to* **Athene**)   I will not be able to protect him from Poseidon's rage, when he returns.

Athene *acknowledges.*

Zeus (*to* **Hermes**)   Go tell the goddess, go tell her that her time, her time with her mortal lover is over.

Hermes *nods . Soundscape – knitting.*

Scene Four

Calypso *enters. The small doll figure of* **Odysseus** *remains on the small island.*

Hermes *approaches* **Calypso**. *He sits quietly with her. They then turn in unison towards the small male figure on the island.*

Calypso   I will not let him go. You cannot make me. I will not let Odysseus go.

Hermes   It is not I who is asking.

Silence.

Calypso   I saved him. He would be walking with the shades if it were not for me. You other gods, Athene too, you did not save him. I saved his life – washed up on my shore – tossed by Poseidon's rage.

Hermes   It is the Cloud Gatherer that asks, Zeus himself asks with the power of his lightning and damnation of his thunderbolt, he asks lovely goddess, lovely Calypso – I am only the messenger.

Calypso   With what ease you slide from responsibility, weaving out of the line of my temper – you gods have always envied the intimacy of mortal man and immortal woman. He is my love.

Hermes   But you are not his. You have held him here for eight years, Calypso.

Calypso   He wished to stay.

Hermes   Who could resist your glittering self, the sight of your skin, the warmth of your passion? But now he weeps at the shore side for his home, his wife, his son. Love him and in loving him set him free.

Calypso (*angrily*)   I will not help him. I will not provide a ship, or supplies or anything to help him on his way.

Hermes *produces a bunch of flowers from a sleeve and presents them to her.*

Hermes   As you wish ageless Calypso, radiant Calypso. But you will let him go.

Calypso *nods.* **Hermes** *exits.*

Calypso *turns towards the small doll figure. Soundscaping – of distant crying – resumes.* **Calypso** *talks to self.*

Calypso   Go home, go home my beloved Odysseus, back to Ithaca.

The crying stops. Soundscape – knitting.

Scene Five

Fate 1
Breathe breath my heart into knitting.
Knitting lifelines.

Fate 2   The Way of the World.

Fate 3   The Wheel of Fortune.

Fate 1   The Weather in the Streets.

All Fates   Pearl one, knit one, pearl one, knit one.

Possibly repeat.

Soundscape – thunder. As the **Fates** *speak, they walk towards the island; one holds a watering can.*

Fate 1   Calypso makes him a boat.

Fate 2   Fills it with wine and food.

Fate 3   Kisses him.

Fate 2   Loves him for the last time.

Fate 1   And sends him on his way.

Fate 2   Out into the sea.

Fate 3   Where the wind blows.

Fate 1   Where the wind howls.

Fate 2   Into a storm.

*The **Fates** blow on the figure on the island, and water it with the watering can. Soundscape of storm and thunder. **Fate 3** knocks the figure off the island.*

Scene Six

Phaeacia. Soundscape – seashore in distance – birds – idyllic.
***Nausicaa** and her **Maids** enter – they carry white sheets, they soak them in the 'moat' and wash them vigorously, thrashing them against the sides. They sing as they wash. **Odysseus** enters, battered, wearing ragged clothes, he is virtually naked. The singing abruptly stops and the **Maids** run and hide. **Nausicaa** stands her ground, nervously fearless.*

Nausicaa   Who are you and what do you want?

*Silence. **Odysseus** stands motionless. Silence as **Nausicaa** awaits a response.*

Nausicaa   Who are you and what do you want of us?

Odysseus *moves towards her, she reacts by moving back.*

Nausicaa   We are a peaceful people, protected and blessed by the gods, favourites of Poseidon. There is no harm here.

Odysseus *mouths words unable to speak.*

Nausicaa   Are you bringer of harm or good?

Odysseus   Good.

Odysseus *collapses on to his knees. He is exhausted.*

Nausicaa   Clothe yourself, man.

Nausicaa *throws a sheet to him.*

Tell me who you are.

Odysseus *can barely answer and finds the retelling of his plight (which is a lie) difficult.*

Odysseus   Aethon, my name is Aethon, from Crete . . .
My crew were reckless . . . the Nile . . . They stole women
and children from the Egyptians. There was an ambush and
we were forced to set sail in a storm. A bad storm, all lost.

Nausicaa   Aethon, stop. You distress yourself. Wash and
clean yourself, we will provide clothes for you. (*To* **Maids**.)
Why are you hiding, come out, all of you and help this
wounded man.

Three of the **Maids** *nervously approach to help* **Odysseus**.

Nausicaa You are the guests of the Phaeacians, Sir. We
live at the world's edge. A peaceful race that know no
enemies. Our city is above the hill, a high wall with tall
towers enclosing it. We are good sailors with fast ships,
speeded by the blessing of the god of the sea. The road that
leads to my father's house winds through orchards of pears,
pomegranates; these trees never fail and burst full of their
fruits throughout the year. We will guide you there, into the
halls of my father. Tell him your story, for I know he will
welcome you as a guest.

Odysseus   Thank you for helping a luckless wanderer.

Nausicaa   You are clearly a man of breeding, Sir.
Perhaps in this small blessed country, of timeless warmth,
you will find substance enough to stay and your luck to
change. But walk a little way behind us Sir, it would be
unseemly if you were seen walking beside Princess Nausicaa,
daughter of King Alcinous, and her maids.

Nausicaa *and* **Maids** *exit.* **Odysseus** *follows.*

Scene Seven

*The feast at Phaeacia. Early evening. All the cast sit casually about the
stage, sharing picnics. They are listening to* **Demodocus** (*the local
storyteller*) *who is entertaining them with a story.* **Odysseus** *is*

among them; sitting near to him are **Nausicaa** *and* **Alcinous**. **Demodocus** *begins mid-tale.*

Demodocus   Hephaestus, furious at his wife Aphrodite's betrayal, returned to his foundry.

All night the clanging and pounding of his anvil on heated iron, echoed through heaven, chains shaped through rage, heated with revenge. In the morning he carried his fine work of vengeance to their bed and hung it high above their mating ground. Aries, carved in male beauty, sought his love in the pink fingers of dawn and Aphrodite, arching with longing, reached her arms out to her love and lay with him. And down fell the iron chains, the mass of Hephaestus's limping rage, the lovers trapped, unable to move from his metal reins.

Then Hephaestus invited all the Olympian gods to come and see Aphrodite lying in bed with Aries. Zeus, Hermes and Apollo laughed, and openly envied Aries, even chained fast to the lovely Aphrodite. But Poseidon did not laugh and begged for Aries' release, that he would ensure his recompense. Hephaestus relented and set both free, Aries under Poseidon's guard to be released later, with no service ever paid, and Aphrodite to her altar in Paphos to be anointed and cleansed from the prying eyes of those male gods.

All clap.

Alcinous   Demodocus, a story well told as ever. Tell us another. Tell us one to entertain our guest. Tell us a story of fighting perhaps, Demodocus.

Nausicaa   A vivid story.

Alcinous   A story of action and strong warring men. Troy. Tell us of Troy.

Demodocus   Wise King Alcinous, Princess Nausicaa, I shall tell you the story of the fall of Troy.

The clever Greeks, led by Odysseus's cunning, hide in their wooden shell – inside the Wooden Horse. The Trojans are sleeping – all night they have been drinking, and feasting, because the Greek camps are empty, desolate, and they believe those warring men have gone. A sign from Agamemnon, a sign from Helen and Odysseus opens the trapped door in the belly of the wooden beast. Under night they slip into the unguarded houses of the sleeping Trojans, slit the throats of the sleeping men, the sleeping infants and force the women. The screaming begins.

Hecabe runs with her daughters. Odysseus had promised her, had promised that those Trojans who did not resist the Greeks would be spared, but the screaming women and children put ice-cold fear in her heart. She hid with her daughters under an ancient laurel tree, near Zeus's altar in the courtyard, pulling her frail husband, King Priam, with her, begging him not to do battle.

But the bloodied and dead body of their son, Polites, fell before them, and Priam shot a feeble arrow towards the Greeks; he was grabbed, pulled away from his crying wife and daughters, and found later by his wife, Hecabe, butchered, headless, at the tomb of Achilles. The Greeks sought to enslave the sobbing Hecabe – but she, mouthing curses, still present in the lives of those cursed Greeks, turned herself into a black dog and jumped into the pit, where her barking can still be heard in Hades, in Tartarus, despairing of Troy – sacked, mutilated, plundered, the walls razed.

A tiny holocaust.

Alcinous   Stop, Demodocus. What story is this?

Demodocus   It is the story of war.

Alcinous   Where is the warrior in this?

Demodocus   My King, you have never seen war. It is not a noble place, Sir.

Alcinous Is it not?

Nausicaa   No, Father.

Alcinous *addresses* **Odysseus**.

Alcinous Never?

Nausicaa   Rarely.

Alcinous And you Aethon, what do you believe?

Odysseus   It was not like that . . . Troy.

Nausicaa   You were there?

Odysseus   I fought with the others, I fought with the Greeks, with Odysseus.

Reaction of audience.

Bitterness grew on both sides. Ten years, ten years we fought for the return of Helen, whom Paris, son of Priam, stole; they stole her from us, then fell in love with her, and Priam, through his pride, though warned by Cassandra and others, refused to return her. The Trojans would steal into our camps at night, not strong enough, or brave enough, to take the whole camp. They would steal into the camps at night, slit the throat of a companion, of a man dear to us, with family and children at home, and they'd take his head, just his head. So in the morning when we awoke in our tents, a companion, our friend, would be found, his bedding soaked in blood, but only his body left behind, his head taken as a token and stuck on some pathway near to the camp – on a stick for our discovery later that day. (*Referring to a guest.*) It could be your head, or yours, or a friend's. After ten years, you don't believe such people are people, and when you rush the city, you are crazed with hate for them. They are no longer noble, or even human, they are like beasts – deserving slaughter.

Silence.

Nausicaa   And what part did you play, Aethon?

Odysseus   Minor.

Nausicaa   You speak with such authority for a minor part.

Demodocus   You speak with the gift of a storyteller, of a man of wisdom and cunning and with the authority of a god.

Odysseus   I'm not a god.

Nausicaa   But you are not Aethon, are you? You did not mention that Aethon had fought beside Odysseus and had been at Troy.

Euryalus   I recognise you.

Alcinous   Who are you?

Euryalus   I know you.

Alcinous   You know this man, Euryalus?

Euryalus   I traded with those people, I traded with the Trojans. This is Odysseus.

Nausicaa   Is this true? Are you him? Is it?

Euryalus   I went in the day after you sacked the city. What Demodocus says is true, you ravaged everything, you Greek barbarians.

Euryalus *moves in to attack* **Odysseus**; **Nausicaa** *steps in between them.*

Alcinous   We are peaceful people. We are peaceful. This war does not concern us.

Euryalus   What sort of a man leads such barbarians?

Nausicaa   We are a neutral country, that knows no enemies. You are both guests and as such you will respect our ways. Odysseus, you are most welcome. Is he not, Father?

Alcinous   Indeed. Indeed he is. Sit down Euryalus. Sit
down both of you.

Silence – as the assembly settles.

Nausicaa   Would you tell us of your travels?

Alcinous   Tell us. Tell us your stories. If you are not too
tired? It has been ten years since Troy, tell us your journeys,
your feats, your travels.

Odysseus   It's a long tale.

Alcinous   We have all night.

Nausicaa   Tell us where you went – after you sailed from
Troy?

All wait – for **Odysseus**'s *response. Possible soundscaping change
beneath text.*

Odysseus   Boiling from the spoil of Troy, burning from
the blood of others, we landed on Ismarus, we sacked, stole
and killed, in the city of the Cicones. But the screams of the
women hurried the men home. We stood firm against them
at first but they broke our line and we fled back to our boats,
booty falling from our arms as we ran.

Odysseus *looks about him. The Phaeacians are silent, clearly
displeased with his line of storytelling.*

Nausicaa   More killing, Odysseus.

Odysseus   Nine days we were at sea, tossed by storms.
Then we saw land, a strange island covered by purple haze.

He abruptly stands up and 'changes his tune'. (Throughout this section
Odysseus *could possibly use bread from the picnic baskets to
represent his* **Men** *or simply use the guests as representations before
they become his* **Men**.)

Odysseus   We landed.

The men, on this island, laughed. They laughed all day
long; nothing seem to hurt them or touch them. It was as if

tomorrow, or the worry of tomorrow, never came. They drank a sickly drink – too sweet for me, made from the juice of the lotus. My men sat with these people and drank all day.

Night came and then dawn and I urged them back to our boats. Then a further day went by, another night, another day. 'Tomorrow,' they'd say, 'do it tomorrow and laugh.' And all the Lotus Eaters would roll and laugh with them and say 'Yes, tomorrow Odysseus, tomorrow, do it then.' Eventually their laziness became unbearable.

Odysseus   We should return.

Man 2   Why?

Odysseus   It is calm. We should get on our way.

Eurylochus   We'll go back tomorrow.

Odysseus   Today, we agreed, today. We've been here for over a week.

Man 1   Drink some of this juice Odysseus, it is sweet.

Odysseus   It is this stuff, this drink the Lotus Eaters have given you, that makes you like this.

Man 3   Like what?

Odysseus   Useless. Do you not want to get home?

Man 3   I'm not useless.

Do you think I'm useless?

Odysseus   Let us go home. You remember home? Ithaca?

Eurylochus (*camply*)   Oh Ithaca.

Odysseus *begins to take either the* **Men** *or the 'bread men', one by one back to the boat. The* **Men** *repeatedly escape pleading with Odysseus as they do so. 'Let us stay', 'I'm not useless', 'Quick, let's go back, while he's not looking', 'Can't we leave tomorrow', 'No, I want* *to stay'. The* **Men** *finally give in. In this chaos the other guests exeunt, leaving only* **Odysseus's Men** *and* **Odysseus** *on stage.*

This jabbering continues until **Odysseus** *binds them all with string. 'Don't tie us up,' 'Can't we just have one more,' 'One more drink for the road?'*

Odysseus   No. I'm setting sail.

So we set sail.

Soundscape – they set sail. **Odysseus** *at the helm. The ship animated within the set. Soundscape – knitting and sea.*

Scene Eight

Fate 3   Oblivion. (*Pause.*) Oblivion we created.

Fate 1   Doom, we created doom.

Fate 2   Disease.

Fate 1   No, that wasn't us.

Fate 3   Pity, we created pity.

Fate 2   Anger.

Fate 3   Terror.

Fate 1   Pride.

Fate 3   Fear.

Fate 2   Longing.

Fate 1   Lies.

Fate 3   Strife.

Pause.

All Fates   And chaos.

Fate 2   No compassion.

Fate 3   Don't say that word, it makes me shudder.

Fate 1   Prometheus moulded, and moulded – little hands and little feet, little heads – with little brains. Took dust from the four corners of the earth: black, brown, red, white. Crackled and turned the being, billowing out its self-importance, with heat, air, and fire.

Fate 3   Till the little pompous things could walk.

Fate 2   And blew humanity, courage, dignity, righteousness.

Fate 3   But not into all of them. Not into those, those . . . footballers, those . . . suitors at Odysseus's palace. Many barbarians, there were many.

Fate 1   That has always been so. The battle of the children of light and the children of darkness.

Fate 3 *cuts off piece of thread.*

Fate 3   One less, one less barbarian.

Fate 2   No compassion?

Fate 3   I've a scarf to finish and several jumpers.

Fate 3   Where is he now?

Fate 2   Returning home, nearing the shores of Ithaca.

Fate 1   No.

Fate 3   No. He's landing where the Cyclops live.

Fate 1   His men are hungry, they've been at sea for days.

Scene Nine

Cyclops *enters – many performers moving as one. One holds an eye above the rest – the performers look with the eye before moving en masse. Soundscape – whispering whenever they move, like a conspiracy. Each performer, within the mass that is* **Cyclops**, *carries pans with milk and curd.*

Fate 1   Lawless things.

Fate 3   Dishevelled in their greed.

The many-handed **Cyclops** *moves his curd and milk from pan to pan – tasting it with his fingers as he does so.*

Fate 2   Ugly one-eyed creature.

Fate 1   Fussing over its cheese.

Cyclops *exits.*

Odysseus *and his* **Men** *enter. The* **Men** *are starving and swoop down on the cheese straight away and start to eat.*

Odysseus   What are you doing?

Man 1   Eating.

Man 2   You should try eating, Odysseus. It's good for you.

Odysseus   We don't know what being is here. We don't know who this belongs too.

Man 3   We're sackers.

Man 1   Sackers of cities.

Eurylochus   No one will mind losing a little cheese.

Man 2   Do a libation.

Man 3   Do a libation to a god.

Man 1   Ask for protection – cheese-makers are unlikely to harm.

Man 4   Curdling and fermenting cheese hardly go hand in hand with serial killing.

Man 1   Cheese-makers – the mass murderers of today.

Odysseus   You are still eating food uninvited.

Man 1   It's delicious; try some.

Eurylochus   Calm yourself and try some.

Eurylochus *holds out some cheese,* **Odysseus** *accepts.*
Cyclops *scuttles in as they are eating. A few* **Men** *have already stopped.* **Odysseus**'s *mouth is dripping with cheese.*

Man 1   What is that?!

Man 2   What sort of monster is that?!

The **Cyclops** *observes them with his one eye as* **Odysseus** *speaks. There is no indication that he can understand them.*

Odysseus   We are Achaeans. We sailed from Troy. We fought alongside Agamemnon.

Silence. **Cyclops** *does not respond, merely twitches his eye and whispers to himself.* **Odysseus** *repeats, more slowly, as if talking to a thing that does not understand English.*

We fought alongside Agamemnon. We have come from Troy and are bound for home.

Cyclops *remains silent – looking.*

Odysseus   We were driven by winds, off course.

Silence – the eye watches. **Odysseus** *kneels.*

I kneel to you Sir, asking the blessings of the gods and welcome of all guests, that Zeus himself protects as god of guests.

Cyclops *finally speaks.*

Cyclops   Do not tell me to be fearful of the gods.

Silence. **Odysseus** *stands.*

Cyclops   Did you like the cheese?

Odysseus   It was excellent.

Odysseus *looks towards his* **Men** *and they nod in agreement: 'Excellent', 'Yes excellent', 'An excellent cheese'. They are clearly terrified.*

Cyclops   Good eh? You all tasted my cheese?

They all nod.

And you tell me to be fearful of the gods, what fool of a country blew life into you? And you steal an honest man's goods, you Zeus-quoting beings. But the cheese was good?

Odysseus   Very.

*All the **Men** repeat: 'Very', 'very'. **Cyclops'** many hands pour out glasses of wine for themselves and drink.*

Cyclops   I often think cheese tastes best followed by a rich wine . . . and flesh.

*Cyclops smiles at the **Men** and **Odysseus** and his **Men** smile back in agreement. **Cyclops** throws down the wine, grabs a **Man** and pulls him into the mass that is the **Cyclops**. **Odysseus** and his **Men** back away in terror. **Cyclops** runs at another **Man** and does the same.*

Cyclops   Please, do not leave my cave. You are my guests. I shall ensure your safety, by sealing the cave with a boulder some twenty men high, and twenty men thick. We will eat together again, later, I am sure. I must milk my goats and pen them in for the night.

*Cyclops exits. **Odysseus** and his **Men** are left, standing in silence – in shock – two of their men dead.*

Eurylochus   He will eat us all. He will eat every one of us. Why didn't you attack him?

Odysseus   What good would it have done? He has the strength of a hundred men. We would all be walking down to Hades now if I had attacked. No, we have to wait.

Man 1   We could rush him.

Odysseus is sharpening a long stick with a knife.

Odysseus   This being will not be 'rushed'. He is no mortal, he is no thing without hindsight.

Eurylochus   We are all lost.

Odysseus   No, Eurylochus, we are not lost. We have not come this far to be lost. We will find a way. Did you bring that wine with you? That good wine?

Eurylochus   Yes.

Odysseus   Give it to me.

Cyclops *enters.* **Odysseus** *and his* **Men** *move away to give him space.* **Cyclops** *drinks some of his milk and then grabs another of the* **Men** – *as before.* **Cyclops** *burps.* **Odysseus** *approaches* **Cyclops** *offering him the wine. As* **Odysseus** *speaks, one of the* **Men** *attempts to sidle out of the cave, clinging onto the sides of the walls as he attempts to sneak out.* **Cyclops** *talks to* **Odysseus** *but as the* **Man** *gets closer to the cave door – the* **Cyclops**' *eye watches him.*

Odysseus   Now you have had your fill of men's flesh, I offer you a libation, and a splendid wine from the spoils of Troy, you who defy the Olympian gods, and Zeus's thunder. I am in awe, in reverence of your strength and of your appetite.

Cyclops *grabs the wine and drinks it, quickly* – *it spills over the sides of his mouth. The* **Man** *sneaking along the side of the cave makes a dash for the entrance.* **Cyclops** *sees him and pulls him into the mass that is the* **Cyclops**.

Cyclops   A good wine. More.

Odysseus *pours* **Cyclops** *more wine* – *he gulps it down once more.*

Cyclops   This wine is *very* good. More please, guest.

Cyclops *attempts to grab a* **Man** *but fails* – *growing sleepy due to the wine.*

Cyclops   What is your name, guest? For you shall be the last I eat amongst your friends.

Odysseus   No-man. My name is No-man. Another glass, defiant god?

Cyclops *puts his goblet out to be refilled. The* **Cyclops** *sits, drinks all of it and then lies back – releasing several loud burps.*

Cyclops   A fine wine, No-man. A fine wine.

Cyclops' *eye rolls across the floor away from the body of the beast.* **Odysseus** *skewers it with the stick he sharpened. The* **Cyclops** *awakes, howling in agony.* **Cyclops** *reels from one side of the cave to another – unable to see.*

Odysseus   Quick, go – as he reels from the pain. Go, all. I will stay distracting him with noise.

Eurylochus   But what of you?

Odysseus   Go.

The **Men** *scurry past the reeling* **Cyclops**, *just missing them with his many arms as they sneak out the entrance at the back of the space and exeunt.*

Cyclops   You will pay a rich price for this, No-man. We are many, we Cyclops, many. I have only to roar and my brothers will come and devour you.

Soundscape – **Cyclops** *roars – enormously loud and howling.* **Odysseus** *runs past him as he roars. From the back of the space, several single eyes appear, all held by a single hand. They look into the space and speak off stage. More eyes appear as the scene continues but never whole bodies.*

Cyclops 1   What is it brother?

Cyclops 2   Why do you shout?

Cyclops   I'm blinded.

Cyclops 3   Did someone blind you, brother?

Cyclops   No-man blinded me.

Cyclops 4   No man blinded you?

Cyclops   Yes, it was No-man.

Cyclops 5   Who blinded him?

Cyclops 1   No man blinded him.

Cyclops 5   I have sheep to attend to.

Cyclops 2   Did you blind yourself then, brother?

Cyclops   No, No-man did.

Cyclops 1   I have cheese to make.

They begin to leave.

Cyclops 3   How careless of you to lose your eye.

Cyclops 4   How can you see now?

Cyclops 3   How careless to lose it to no man.

Cyclops 4   Come brothers, I've some curdling to finish.

Cyclops   Where are you going? No, no – you must go after No-man. No, don't go, brothers.

All eyes have now gone from the entrance to the cave. Off stage.

Cyclops 2   How careless he is.

Cyclops 1   How careless to lose an eye to no man.

Possible backdrop of **Odysseus** *sailing on his ship with his* **Men**. *Soundscape – knitting.*

Scene Ten

As the **Fates** *speak, sound of rooms full of laughter and feasting; a party is in full swing.*

Fate 1
And they land.

Fate 2
On the Aeolian Isles.

Fate 3
Aeolus.

Fate 1
Laughter filling this place with its high bronze walls
And secret passages, twisting up to the
Palace of laughter.
Aeolus, keeper of the winds.

Fate 3
The disease carrying Southern winds.

Fate 2
The sands carrying Eastern winds.

Fate 1
The welcome North wind, bringing rain from the cold.

Fate 2
The West wind he releases for Odysseus's journeying.
Sending the men, bellies full, on their way.

Fate 3
With a gift. A bag containing all the winds of the sea.

A door opens slightly – a party can be seen through the slim gap. King **Aeolus** *is talking to* **Odysseus**. *As they talk they come into the main space of the stage.*

Aeolus   A Cyclops you say. Odysseus, your stories make us laugh, you escaped one with a sharp stick?

Odysseus   Yes, through the eye. I blinded him.

Aeolus   Impossible, tall tales.

Odysseus   No, King Aeolus, he is blinded.

Aeolus   The Cyclops has the strength of a hundred men.

Odysseus   I blinded him.

Aeolus   For your own sake, I hope your story is untrue. We have the same father, the Cyclops and I, that's why he proved so fearless, so mocking of the Cloud Gatherer, of Zeus himself. We are the Earthshaker's son, the maker of the winds, the rains – the god of the Sea, Poseidon. This, Odysseus –

Odysseus's Men *enter and begin to set up ship on the stage, hoisting up the sail. They are oblivious of* **Odysseus***'s and* **Aeolus***'s chat.*

Aeolus   – this is your journey home, across the wild, wild seas – a forest of unexpected passions: storms, gales, howlings of lost things, stir in this endless water. This is your path home. Poseidon, our father, will not forgive you for blinding his son and these territories, this wilderness sea, is his.

He hands him a small red velvet bag which moves.

Here, take this bag. It is a bag containing all the winds – I have released the West wind for you – to send you on your way. Take this bag with you.

Aeolus *moves away to exit.*

And safe journeying, my entertaining friend.

All exeunt. The bag is left centre stage – moving. Soundscape – a ship being put to sea. The **Men** *sing as they set up and sail.*

Men 1–6
Splice the main brace, haul up the sheets
Lift the anchor below
Hold the tiller, furl up the sails
Fix your eyes on the horizon.

At sea. The bag, now still, sits centre stage. **Man 1** *notices the bag.*

Man 1   What's this?

Eurylochus   It's the present King Aeolus gave to Odysseus.

Man 1   Where is Odysseus now?

Eurylochus   He's sleeping.

Silence. They all look at the bag.

Man 2   It's gold isn't it? So typical of him to take all the glory himself and not spread it about.

Man 1   I received no gift from Aeolus.

Eurylochus   Is it typical of him? Of Odysseus?

Man 3   We should share it out.

Man 4   It's as much his as ours.

Eurylochus   I'm sure he intended to share.

Man 2   Loyal Eurylochus, your devotion makes you blind to his wiles, his storytelling.

Eurylochus   We are nearly home, perhaps it is for us when we reach home. I believe we are about two days' journeying from Ithaca, maybe less.

Man 2   Why would he deal it out later? Why would he hold on to it till then? I say we share it out now, while he sleeps. We'll leave a share for him inside.

Eurylochus   I still think you should consider.

Man 1 (*picking up bag*)   Gold, Eurylochus – or better – gems, gems that contain the Sun if held up to the eye, placed on a wife's finger or round her slender much-missed neck. What else would you keep in a (*Opening bag.*) velvet bag . . .

The force of the winds rushing out of the bag blows him backwards. Soundscape – sound of howling winds. Storm. **Odysseus** *awakes and rushes on deck.*

Odysseus   What have you done?! What have you done?! We're turning around, we're turning away from home.

He sees the open bag on the floor.

You opened the bag. You've released the sea winds – all of them.

Odysseus *shouts instructions at them – to prepare for a storm. Possibly soundscape as the wind howls louder and louder. Sound of tearing sails, men shouting out. Blackout.*

Scene Eleven

Soundscape – birds and seashore.

Odysseus *and his* **Men** *lie about the stage. Slowly illuminated – dawn.* **Eurylochus** *is sitting up.* **Odysseus** *is sleeping on the side of the stage near* **Eurylochus**. *The* **Men** *stir.*

Man 1   How near were we?

Eurylochus   About two days.

Soundscape – sound of music in distance – discordant, unearthly. One by one the **Men** *exit – drawn by the music.*

Man 2   How far from home are we now?

Eurylochus   I don't know where we are. But it seems peaceful enough. Some god or goddess, perhaps, guided us here.

Man 1   I'm so hungry . . .

Man 2   If it hadn't been for you, we'd be home by now.

Man 1   How long were we tossed by the storms? Night and day seemed one – in the gapless sea.

Eurylochus   Five days and five nights.

Man 1   Is he sleeping?

Eurylochus   Yes. He was up before the rest of us, searching for food.

Man 1 *and* **Eurylochus** *are the last to leave. They wander off towards the end of their dialogue, becoming very distracted as the music mounts in volume.*

Man 1   Did he find any?

Eurylochus   Yes, yes . . . there's some wild boar . . . over the hills . . .

Circe *enters.* **Odysseus's Men** *sit watching, transfixed by her.*
As they re-enter the space, **Circe's Attendants** *hand each one a*
goblet of wine and offer a choice of fruit, mostly grapes.

Circe   Eat. Stay. You are most welcome.

More of **Odysseus's Men** *enter one by one.*

Circe's Attendant 1   Eat.

Circe's Attendant 2   Stay.

Circe's Attendant 3   You are most welcome.

They repeat almost as a round as each of the **Men** *enter – and*
continue to offer wine and fruit to each.

Circe's Attendant 1   Eat.

Circe's Attendant 2   Stay.

Circe's Attendant 3   You are most welcome.

Etc.

Athene *and* **Hermes** *enter.* **Odysseus** *awakes.*

Odysseus   Where are my men?

Athene   With Circe.

Hermes   A dark goddess, visitor of the Shades.

Circe (*to* **Men**)   More, would you like more?

Circe's Attendant 1   More?

Circe's Attendant 2   More?

Circe's Attendant 3   Would you like more?

The **Attendants** *repeat, as they talk to each guest, as in a round.*
The **Attendants** *continue to offer more wine and fruit as they speak.*
One of the **Men** *begins to twitch, a little at first and then violently –*
just with his head and then with the whole of his body – shutting his
eyes as if in pain. The other **Men** *turn to watch him.* **Circe** *and her*
Attendants *stop offering wine. The* **Man** *buckles over – on to his*

*arms, so he is on all fours. Another begins to twitch, following the same
pattern of behaviour; all the* **Men** *turn to watch.*

*He too doubles over with pain and ends up on all fours. They begin to
grunt.* **Circe** *has turned them into pigs.* **Circe** *and her*
Attendants *herd them off the stage. The women speak together as
they do: 'Here piggy, piggies', 'Here piggy, piggies', 'Come swine, move
along', 'Here little piggies'.*

Odysseus   What has she done with them?

Eurylochus *enters out of breath and terrified.*

Athene   She has turned them into pigs.

Eurylochus   Pigs! She has turned them into pigs.

Eurylochus *falls silent – equally terrified in the presence of the
gods.*

Athene   She means to sacrifice them.

Odysseus   She means to sacrifice my men? When did
they wander off? Why is it that I just have to fall asleep and
they make trouble?

Eurylochus (*still very nervous*)   The music . . . the music.
We all followed it, we couldn't help ourselves and she is
so . . . beautiful.

Hermes   She shimmers, it's true.

Athene   She will harm you too.

Hermes   She is powerful. We will arm you against her.

Eurylochus   I'm not going back, and you can't make me.

Athene   We will arm you.

Eurylochus   I'm not going.

Hermes   I will give you a herb, a herb that is resistant to
Circe's spells. You may taste her wine and her food, but
when she touches you with her hand, take the knife from
your side and hold it to her throat. She will submit.

Athene   But do not trust her. She will wish to lie with you. Let her.

Hermes   Let her. It is her prerogative.

Athene   As a goddess. Do not refuse her, but before you lie with her make her take an oath she will do you no more mischief.

Hermes   Or she will kill you . . . after.

Athene (*to* **Odysseus**)   Go.

Odysseus *turns to leave.*

Eurylochus   I'm not going.

Athene   Go, free your men.

Hermes *and* **Athene** *exeunt.*

Eurylochus   I'm not going back there.

Odysseus   Stay here Eurylochus, you can look after the ship. Wash up perhaps?

Odysseus *exits.*

Scene Twelve

Soundscape – **Circe**'s *music.* **Circe** *enters with her* **Attendants**. *The* **Attendants** *perform as before – offering wine and fruit to* **Odysseus** *when he enters.*

Circe's Attendant 1   Eat.

Circe's Attendant 2   Stay.

Circe's Attendant 3   You are most welcome.

Odysseus *sits and watches, enraptured.* **Circe's Attendants** *offer him more.*

Circe's Attendant 1   More?

Circe's Attendant 2   More?

Circe's Attendant 3   Would you like more?

Odysseus *accepts and happily drinks.* **Circe** *goes to turn* **Odysseus** *into a pig, but* **Odysseus** *grabs her and places a knife at her throat.*

Circe   Strange man, release me. I will do you no harm. No one has ever defied my herbs. No one. Lie with me, hold me in those arms, and let an ocean of longing fill your being.

Odysseus   I will join you, yes, I will join you in your bed . . . yes. (*Falling for her.*) Yes.

Circe *leads him off;* **Odysseus** *comes to his senses.*

Odysseus   But first . . .

Circe *strokes his arm with one finger, distracting him.*

Circe   Yes, my love.

Odysseus *melts.* **Circe** *continues stroking his arm.* **Odysseus** *recovers.*

Odysseus   But first.

Circe   Yes, my man of fine glistening flesh.

Odysseus *continues to melt.* **Odysseus** *recovers.*

Odysseus   Firstly!

Circe   Man of the long, long night. Come with me.

Odysseus *begins to move off stage again with her and then recovers once more.*

Odysseus   An oath.

Circe   An oath?

Odysseus   An oath.

Circe *strokes his arm again, he melts again but quickly recovers.*

Odysseus   An oath before lovemaking.

Circe (*acting bored*)   A solemn one?

Odysseus   Yes.

Circe *yawns.*

Circe   An oath. Such a passion killer, oaths.

Circe *moves her finger up his neck again.* **Odysseus** *melts and quickly resists.*

Circe   Wouldn't you rather simply 'take me'.

Odysseus   An oath.

Circe   Suddenly I am *so* tired. I think I have a headache coming on.

Odysseus   I need an oath. Please. Please?

Circe   To do you no harm, I suppose?

Odysseus   Yes.

Circe   And to release your men, I suppose?

Odysseus   Yes.

Circe   Oh all right. 'In the folds of our desire, I grant you both.'

Circe *shouts back at her* **Attendants** *without looking at them as she drags the willing* **Odysseus** *away.*

Circe   Release the pigs. We're going to bed.

Scene Thirteen

Odysseus *and* **Circe** *sit folded around each other.* **Circe's Attendants** *sit with* **Odysseus's Men**, *relaxed and drinking.* **Odysseus** *sighs, repeatedly.*

Circe   You sigh?

Odysseus   Yes I sigh.

Circe   Why do you sigh? When you have everything here.

Odysseus   I want to go home.

Circe   Oh mortals, they're so . . . domestic. You offer them the world of enchantment, beauty beyond compare, violins at dawn, at night, in the middle of the day, late afternoon. Drapes, you give them drapes, hung with celestial flair, very tasteful – but no, they'd always rather go home. Tell me, Odysseus, what is this home?

Odysseus   It is where living begins, where identity, strength, courage is gathered – the source of home. And inside me, my beloved goddess, there are still the deaths of my kinsmen and the violence of Troy, sitting within me. At home I believe that wandering within shall end, and the return will cleanse me. Home is the taste of self again.

Circe   War is natural, is it not? It is natural to defend one's own, to retrieve what's stolen.

Odysseus   No, it is not natural, it is not natural to kill another man.

Circe   You know, I just can't see that, killing men seems so natural to me. I mean it helps if you turn them into pigs first, and they taste better.

Silence.

There, I've made you angry. You all seem so troubled to me you mortals, fragile things, full of fragments of being. And you think Ithaca will make you whole again. Yes, of course, go home then. But first you would be ill advised to travel without guidance. Poseidon, the Earthshaker, the trident-bearing keeper of the sea still pursues you. I cannot see your fortune clearly. You must descend to Hades, to Tartarus, to ask guidance from the Theban seer, Teiresias himself.

Odysseus   To Hades?

Circe   Yes, Odysseus, to Hades.

Odysseus   How can I return from such a place?

Circe   I will give you herbs, a peace-meal for Cerberus, the many-headed dog that guards the Underworld, and payments for Charon the Ferryman to cross the River Styx. I will give you magic for all but without the Theban seer's guidance I fear you will never reach home. The trial of a descent to Hades must be taken Odysseus, if you are ever to see your precious Ithaca again.

Soundscape – knitting. **Circe**, **Odysseus** *and his* **Men** *exeunt.*

Scene Fourteen

Odysseus *and his* **Men** *sail.*

Men 1–6 (*sing*)
Splice the main brace, haul up the sheets
Lift the anchor below
Hold the tiller, furl up the sails
Fix your eyes on the horizon.

Fate 1
Moving in the mist they sail.

Fate 2
To an island of marsh lands.

Fate 1
They anchor. His men stay by the boat.
Odysseus alone treads where the living dare not walk.

Men *exit.*

Fate 2
Forever at dusk this place,
Water heard beneath the ground.

Fate 3
Black poplars line the entrance within.
A way in, with Circe's potions.
Thrown up, up into the air,
Potions of blood,

Of sacrifice,
Of killing
And the way splits open
Down to the pit where the rivers run black.

Soundscape – rivers and dogs barking in the distance. **Odysseus**
enters Hades.

Fate 2   The river of lamenting.

Fate 3   The river of fire.

Fate 1   The river of woe.

Fate 2   And Lethe.

Fates 2 *and* **3**   Lethe . . .

Fates 1 *and* **2**   The river of forgetting.

Fate 1   And Tartarus itself, bound, tied by the hated river
of the Styx.

Soundscape – aggressive and loud barking of a number of dogs.
Charon *approaches* **Odysseus** *with* **Cerberus** *on a leash.*
Odysseus *backs away.* **Cerberus** *corners* **Odysseus**.
Odysseus *manoeuvres around the space trying to avoid*
Cerberus. *The three-headed dog eventually corners him.*
Odysseus *puts his hand in his pocket and throws golden dust into
the air – the dog falls silent and drifts into sleep.*

Odysseus *negotiates with* **Charon**, *opening a box full of gold and
gems.*

Odysseus   A gift?

Odysseus *moves closer to the river.*

Charon   Do you think such trinkets are enough for a
living man to cross the Styx? What arrogance fills you, what
pride fills your bones. This river is not travelled through
gold, or precious stones, but by the payment of life itself.
Go, idiot, go back to the living.

Charon *turns and moves back to the other shore.*

Odysseus *takes a handful of white dust from his pocket and throws it over the Styx.*

Odysseus Goddess of Death, Circe – hear me and my frozen wish.

The river freezes. Soundscape.

Ferryman, I have no need of your boat. I shall skate across your river.

As **Odysseus** *skates,* **Charon** *exits and the* **Shades** *enter, including* **Teiresias** *and* **Anticleia**. *The* **Shades** *carry themselves with great sadness, constantly and slowly pacing about the place. Only* **Odysseus** *is still. He spots* **Teiresias** *and stops him.*

Odysseus Teiresias? Teiresias?

Teiresias Son of Laertes, Odysseus, why are you here? Leave this unhappy place, go back to the living, lest you be caught.

Odysseus Circe sent me, she sent me to speak to you. I wish to go home. She says the path back is treacherous and only you as seer of the past, future and present can guide me home.

Teiresias I see. You want me to look for you. You blinded his son. He's revenge bubbling at the bottom of the sea – thick he is with it. Yes, I see. Three. There are three first.

Odysseus Three?

Teiresias Monsters they are. The first are the most beautiful but not to be heard, the Sirens – their song so vivid, so wanton, that they tempt men to death on the rocks; you must not listen to their song or your men will die on those rocks. You must pass the straits of the Scylla and the Charybdis. The Scylla, half rock, half woman, sail close to her side; she has many heads and many arms and she will grab you and your men and throw them against the rock.

But do not think of sailing away from her side, for in that strait lives the Charybdis, more dreadful still; she is a whirlpool that drains the sea to its bed and then floods the straits with her water again. There is no surviving her and the only path is to sail close to man-grabbing Scylla.

Anticleia *stops moving and watches* **Odysseus** *and* **Teiresias**.

Teiresias　But further places of warning are, yes, the island of Helios's cattle. You must not eat any of these divine cattle, owned by Helios, the god of the Sun. If you or any of your men eat these creatures, then you will never reach home.

His prophecy over, **Teiresias** *comes out of his trance-like state, unable to remember what he has said.*

Yes, Odysseus, what did you want? You were asking for a prediction.

Odysseus　And you gave it.

Teiresias　I did?

Odysseus　Yes.

Teiresias　But you should go back, leave this unhappy place and go back to the living.

Teiresias *joins the other* **Shades** *and begins to pace once more.* **Anticleia** *approaches* **Odysseus**.

Odysseus (*whispering*)　How are you here? How are you here?

Anticleia　How I've missed you.

Odysseus　When did you reach here? When did you?

Anticleia　Your father attends his fruit trees every day, barely going to your palace, wandering, aching with age, and grieving the loss of his son.

Penelope, she remains pining too, beset by suitors, who squander your riches and your son, Telemachus, wise and strong he is now.

Odysseus   And you, what brought you here?

Anticleia   A broken heart, my son. I missed your gentleness too much. I missed your voice and I thought you dead.

Odysseus   Gentleness?

Anticleia   Yes gentle, calming ways. When you left I felt certain you would never return and that gentle manner would not be seen by me once more, but here you are. Go home, find your grieving father, Laertes, hold him and love him.

Odysseus   Will you hold me? Will you hold me?

The **Shades** *begin to gather around* **Odysseus** *and his mother.*

Anticleia   The sinews, the muscles, the flesh, dear son, are no longer attached to the bones and are at the mercy of fire. No dark blood holds and tends my form. Once all breathing life has gone, it is as if the spirit takes flight, and is near – but hovering – away from the self. Odysseus, there is no self to hold, we are shadows – shades of ourselves. Return to the living before the Styx warms and your frozen pathway home melts.

Odysseus *is now surrounded by the* **Shades***; they block his path. Soundscape – knitting.* **Anticleia** *talks underneath the* **Fates'** *dialogue.*

Anticleia   Let him go. Let my son go. Let the great Odysseus pass. Let him pass. Let him pass.

Odysseus *pushes past the* **Shades***.*

Fate 2
Then he's running.

Fate 1
Running.

Fate 3
Pushing through the Shades.

Fate 2
The Shades try to touch
His skin, feel for the heart beating
Inside, the terror within.

Fate 1
The trembling of life at their finger tips.

Fate 3
Hoping their hovering spirits might sense
The walls of the living again.

Fate 2
Then he's running.

Fate 1
Running.

Soundscape – **Odysseus** *running and out of breath. Soundscape – rushing river and* **Cerberus***'s barking.* **Odysseus***'s breathing increases in volume as he escapes Hades.*

Fate 3
Pushing through the Shades.

Fate 1
From the ruins of the Asphodel Fields.

Fate 2
Over the melting Styx.

Fate 3
He stumbles and falls. Clawing the banks,
Past the barking demon of the pit.

Fate 2
Feeling terror.
Run, Odysseus, run.

Fate 1
Run.

Fate 3
Lest the night might catch hold of you.
Lest the floor of Hades
Shut tight and pull you
To the fields,
To the fields,
To the Asphodel Fields –
There to wander for eternity.

Fate 2
Then he's running.

Fate 1
Running.

Fate 3
Pushing through the night.

Soundscape – external – the sea. **Men 1–6** *enter.*

Fate 1
Out on to the open land.

Fate 2
Over the marshland.

Fate 3
To the sea, to the sea.

Soundscape – **Odysseus** *and his* **Men** *set sail.*

Men 1–6 (*sing*)
Splice the main brace, haul up the sheets
Lift the anchor below
Hold the tiller, furl up the sails
Fix your eyes on the horizon.

•

Scene Fifteen

Odysseus *and his* **Men** *are on the deck of the ship.* **Odysseus** *is sitting moulding something (wax) in his hands.*

Odysseus   Can you see anything ahead?

Eurylochus   Nothing.

Odysseus   There should be twin rocks, near now.

Eurylochus   Nothing.

Man 1   There, Eurylochus, starboard. Twin rocks.

Man 4   There King Odyssues – starboard. Black they are, black and empty.

Odysseus (*to* **Man 1**)   Come here. (**Odysseus** *places wax in his ears.*)

Man 2   What are you doing?

Odysseus   Placing wax in your ears.

Man 2   I don't want wax in my ears.

Odysseus   And you Eurylochus, you must bind me firmly to the mast as soon as there is wax in all your ears. Bind me tightly and firmly, so there is no escape.

Eurylochus   What new trick is this?

Man 2   Can't hear anything now.

Odysseus   Those two rocks are where the Sirens live. Such is the sublime beauty of their song, so irresistible to men, we will sail our ship nearer and nearer to the rocks, to hear still more of their spell-binding singing. Until our bow is crushed and we are broken on those deadly rocks. They bewitch men, drive them mad with their song.

All the **Men** *grab the wax from* **Odysseus**'s *hands, rapidly.*

Odysseus   Tie me quickly to the mast. I want to hear them.

They tie him to a pillar and hurriedly place wax in their ears. As the last **Man** *places wax in his ears, there is utter silence.* **Odysseus** *moves his head from side to side – as if listening to music, like a lullaby to begin with, then reacting to the music as if sublime, then finally so beautiful it is as if he is in pain and tries to break the ties but is unable.*

Eurylochus *watches him and runs in fear, ready to secure the ties when* **Odysseus** *tries to break through and is then still, defeated by the binds and the beauty of the song. When movement is finished and he is still, the* **Fates** *talk softly. They do not knit, putting down their needles for a moment.* **Odysseus** *is untied.*

Fate 2
And he heard the Sirens' song.

Fate 3
They bend the hovering soul to lust,
Devour, senseless on those rocks
Men twisted out in blistered blue.

Fate 2
And he heard the Sirens' song.

Fate 1
And he will ache

Fate 2
Ache for the call

Fate 3
To pass by that beauty one more moment

Fate 2
That vicious hard of ravished song.

The **Fates** *knit. Soundscape – knitting, followed by sea.*

Scene Sixteen

The **Men** *and* **Odysseus** *are going about their chores – manning the ship.*

Men 1–6 (*sing*)
Splice the main brace, haul up the sheets
Lift the anchor below
Hold the tiller, furl up the sails
Fix your eyes on the horizon.

The wind drops. The **Men** *stop singing.* **Odysseus** *and his* **Men** *are surrounded in mist.*

Odysseus   Through the straits. Up ahead. Yes, that's it, guide her steady.

Man 4   I can't see, I can't see where we're going. The mist is too thick.

Odysseus   That's it, guide her near the rocks. Guide her, guide her. Calmly now, calmly now. Nearing home. Take her closely by the rocks.

Man 1   I saw something move.

Odysseus   Close to the rock.

Man 1   It moved, the rock moved.

Soundscape – faint sound of roaring ahead, somewhere between sea and monster (the **Charybdis***).*

Odysseus   Stick close to her.

Man 1   It moved, it moved again.

Man 2   It's moving. The rock's moving.

Odysseus   Stick close to her!

Eurylochus   And the noise, Odysseus, what is that noise?

Sound of roaring increases.

Odysseus   Stay close to the rock and we'll escape.

Man 2   But the rock is moving, the rock is alive.

Numerous hands appear out of the mist, a **Man** *is snatched from the boat. Sound of* **Charybdis** *– mounts towards deafening.*
Odysseus *starts shouting over the sound as do his* **Men***.*

Eurylochus   She has taken one of us. Move away from the rock.

Odysseus   No, keep her close.

Eurylochus   The rock is alive, Odysseus. We should move further out.

Odysseus   No. There lies the Charybdis. She will kill us all just surely as the Scylla grabs a few.

Eurylochus   Pitiless man, how I curse the day I set sail to Troy with you.

Soundscape – noise of the **Charybdis** *takes over – shouts and screaming from the* **Men***.*

Man 3   I'm taking her out.

Odysseus   No, no.

Man 3   I'm taking her away from this monster, she's taking our crew. I'm taking her back out to sea.

Odysseus   No, not to the Charybdis. Pallas, Pallas Athene. If these are the last words I utter, help us, help us. Help these undeserving men who will not listen.

Athene *enters as the boat is about to be dragged down by the sucking* **Charybdis***.* **Odysseus** *and his* **Men** *exeunt once* **Athene** *has taken the ship from them.* **Athene** *guides the ship into safety. Soundscape of* **Charybdis** *fades to nothing – gentle waters and wind take over.* **Athene** *guides the boat into a port.*

Athene
A peaceful isle, this, Odysseus.
Home of the Sun god, Helios's cattle.

Athene *exits but is grabbed by trident-bearing* **Poseidon***.*

Poseidon   Where is he?

Athene   Who?

Poseidon   Your favourite.

Athene   My favourite what?

Poseidon   You, like the more sentimental of the heavenly gods, have favourites amongst this piteous pile – humanity.

Athene   You have favourites, Uncle.

Poseidon   Where have you hidden him?

Athene   I have not 'hidden' him, because he has done nothing wrong, Poseidon.

Poseidon   He blinded my son.

Athene   That reckless one-eyed monster you fathered.

Poseidon   My loyal son.

Athene   Loyal to you and barbarian to all else, 'cept his goatherd. You'll have to find him yourself.

Poseidon   Be in no doubt that I will and be . . . less arrogant, Pallas Athene, you'd do well to remember my birthright and also my dominion, this great ocean, this endless blue on which your Odysseus depends travelling back to his Ithaca. (*Pause.*) You have come from Helios's Isle, haven't you? That is the only island in these blue waters, the island where Helios keeps his precious cattle. Hard it would be to hunger on that isle.

Athene   There is plenty of food there.

Poseidon   For the moment, yes.

Athene   He has more cunning than any match.

Poseidon   But I have more sea Athene, more sea.

Athene *leaves.* **Poseidon** *exits in the opposite direction – via the* '*moat*'.

Soundcape – knitting.

Scene Seventeen

Odysseus's Men *enter – they sit about the place, some chew grass. Soundscape – seashore and seagulls.*

Man 1   Where is he?

Man 2   He's gone up to the mountains to see if he can see a break in the weather.

Eurylochus *enters carrying some barley and some wild fruit.*

Eurylochus   I've found some more wild barley and some fruit.

Man 3   Fruit! What we need is meat, I'm sick of your fruit.

Man 2   Sick of wild grain.

Eurylochus   It's quite a lot of barley.

Man 5   Don't you ache for meat, Eurylochus?

Man 1   Every day we watch these cattle graze.

Man 2   Those splendid thighs.

Man 3   Cutlets.

Man 5   Chops.

Man 6   Those ribs.

Man 1   Kidneys diced and fried.

Man 2   Legs on spits, turning.

Man 5   Every day we watch them graze.

Man 1   Every day for three months.

Eurylochus   Is it three months?

Man 1   You know it's three months.

Man 2   Stuck on this empty isle.

Man 3   And you bring us grain again, Eurylochus.

Man 1   Grain and fruit.

Eurylochus   There must be a break in the weather soon.

Man 1   You know very well that it's some god that keeps us here, with endless storms and winds on this barren place.

Eurylochus   Mhmm. (*Eating.*) This fruit is sweet.

Man 6   Cutlets roasted over the fire till the smell echoes.

Man 1   Chops.

Man 2   Ribs.

Man 3   Legs.

Man 5   Kidneys diced and fried.

Cattle enter.

Eurylochus   These cattle belong to Helios, the god of the Sun. Odysseus has said.

Man 1   'Odysseus has said.'

Man 2   If it wasn't for Odysseus we wouldn't be here at all. It is Odysseus who has angered the gods, not us. It is Odysseus who is the reason why we are stuck here, held by these storms.

Man 5   If we make an offering, an offering praising Helios, make an offering to the god of the Sun, then surely he will not be offended. There are so many cattle here, missing one or two should make no difference to him.

Eurylochus   I'd advise caution, caution against this.

Man 1   Eurylochus, you would advise caution against the world.

Man 6   If we eat it all up before he returns, Odysseus will never know.

*The **Men** pounce on one of the cattle.*

Scene Eighteen

Soundscape – knitting. Followed by the sea. Soundscape – setting sail.
Men *on stage manning their posts at sea.*

Odysseus   It was as stormy as ever, the sea in a swirl, and
then suddenly calm, completely calm, after all these months,
as if a god had been appeased, or forgiven perhaps. Perhaps
a god forgave. So we set sail. How does it look at ahead?

Man 1   Calm.

Man 2   All calm.

Odysseus   Nothing in sight, no twin rocks.

Man 3   No.

Odysseus   No grasping rocks.

Man 5   No.

Odysseus   No whirlpools.

Man 6   None that I can see, Odysseus.

Odysseus   No one-eyed monsters.

Man 1   No.

Odysseus   No pigs.

Eurylochus   No.

Odysseus   And no singers.

The crew relax, possibly laugh. **Poseidon's Attendants** *stand
behind the puppet ship.*

Men 1–6 (*sing*)
Splice the main brace, haul up the sheets
Lift the anchor below
Hold the tiller, furl up the sails
Fix your eyes on the horizon.

Repetition of previous sailing song but in minor key, mounting menace of **Poseidon** *beneath song. Distant thunder breaks their jovial behaviour.* **Poseidon** *enters.*

Poseidon   I have you now. I have you. In your little boat, Odysseus. At night I hear my howling son, at night I watch over him, stumbling in the darkness. And now I have you. I have you now.

Odysseus   I am guarded. I am guarded by those other gods.

Poseidon   No, not any more. You are alone, you and your men.

Soundscape – mounting storm – thunder, louder and nearer. **Athene** *and* **Hermes** *enter.*

Athene   You were warned.

Soundscape – the storm mounts and gets nearer.

Hermes   You were told.

Odysseus   I don't understand. I don't know what has changed.

Athene   I cannot help you.

Hermes   You ate Helios's cattle. You ate the Sun god's cattle.

Athene   I cannot help you.

Odysseus   They were untouched. Untouched by me.

Hermes   Your men, Odysseus.

Odysseus   My men?

Hermes   They killed his cattle. They ate them.

Odysseus   But I know nothing of that, nothing.

Hermes *takes* **Athene** *by the hand and pulls her off.*

Odysseus   Athene! Athene!

Storm.

Odysseus's *words are muffled by an almighty crack of thunder.*
Soundscape – **Odysseus** *continues to shout her name in the mix.*
The most violent storm depicted in the play with extensive thunder and
lightning. Sound of ship being split in two, flooding, chaos.

Soundscape – diminishes in volume and the Phaeacians join him once
more, as in Scene Seven.

Scene Nineteen

The court at Phaeacia. King **Alcinous**, **Nausicaa** *and the rest of*
the cast sit about **Odysseus**, *listening to the end of his story.*

Odysseus   And the sea, it swallowed me. Water washed
its way round every part of my dying self. All of Poseidon's
passion drowning me and drowning the poor dead men.

Nausicaa   And how did you come to survive that
dreadful storm?

Odysseus   A hand came to bury me, to lift me from
silting sands. Calypso, radiant god of the seashore. She
dipped her hand into that dying place and pulled me to
land. She saved me, she saved me, but not my poor dying
men. There they lie at the bottom of the sea, there they lie
in the hands of Scylla, in the coils of Charybdis, in the caves
of the Cyclops, at Troy.

Nausicaa   Tired man.

Odysseus   She has just released me. For eight years she
held me there.

Nausicaa (*referring to* **Odysseus**)   So tired.

Alcinous *claps and all follow.*

Alcinous   Marvellous tales, marvellous tales.

He continues to clap through the scene.

Nausicaa   We must find you a ship, home to Ithaca.

Nausicaa, **Alcinous**, **Odysseus** *and the Phaeacians exeunt.*
Soundscape – knitting.

Scene Twenty

The Magic Shop (Olympus). **Hermes** *and* **Zeus** *are playing with*
some small plastic pigs – grunting. **Athene** *is attempting to do a*
magic trick and failing.

Soundscape – a bang of a door off stage, a door reverberating in a vast
chamber. Footsteps on a wooden, or stone, floor approach, reverberating
down the unseen corridor. Bang as another door slams shut, footsteps
boom louder as they come closer. None of the gods seem remotely
troubled by this noise and continue as before. **Poseidon** *enters,*
furious.

Poseidon   You've released him from Calypso's isle!

Zeus *does not look up from his pigs and responds nonchalantly.*

Zeus   Yes, months gone.

Poseidon (*to* **Zeus**)   I was away, (*To* **Athene**.) you knew,
Pallas Athene, you knew!

Athene *continues trying to attempt her magic trick and does not look*
up.

Athene   Let him go home, Uncle.

Poseidon   At night I watch my blinded child stumble, at
night I hear his pain!

Hermes *starts grunting loudly as the argument escalates.* **Athene**
stops doing her magic trick and turns to address **Poseidon**.

Athene   He's paid enough, Odysseus has paid enough for
the blinding of that unruly giant. Ten years it's been since
that accident.

Poseidon   No accident, vengefully blinded – my son, my blinded son. Tricked and deceived by your favourite. Protected by you, equally bent towards trickery and stealing.

Athene   You flooded those lands of mine, you stole them beneath your watery tongue – they were mine!

Zeus *stops playing with pigs and looks towards them both.*

Poseidon   No they were mine. They were only on loan. You stole them from me!

Athene   No I didn't!

Hermes*' grunting becomes louder and more frequent in response to the argument.*

Poseidon   Yes you did!

Athene   No I didn't!

Penelope   Yes you did!

Athene   No I didn't!

Zeus   Stop it, stop it, both of you. Those land arguments between you both were settled. Hermes stop grunting. Brother, your son is blinded, he dreams of the light of day and for that I am sorry.

But this man, this Odysseus, he has been wandering ten years since and your son, no libations, no duty, no reverence he gave to the heavenly gods here on Olympus. Odysseus by his own cunning and skill defeated your one-hundred-strong child. Odysseus fought in Troy for nine years, and has been wandering, caught, trapped in his ache to return for a further ten. His price is adequate. He has been taken home, by those swift seaman; blessed by you, the Phaeacians, Odysseus sleeps in the bowels of their ship. Punish them for their defiance and let that be enough.

Poseidon   I will not listen to . . .

Zeus   By the power of my thunderbolt you will, Brother! You will listen and you will take heed! Take your punishment of that man elsewhere and let him be.

Soundscape – knitting. **Zeus**, **Athene** *and* **Poseidon** *exeunt.*

Fate 1
Poseidon goes down to the shore.

Fate 2
Waits on the Phaeacian coast.
Waves curl at his side, roam about him, watching.

Fate 1
The good ship returns.
The best men, the fastest ship, the Phaeacians own.

Fate 2
And there, on the shore
As Nausicaa, as Alcinous watch, as the Phaeacians watch,
The ship reaches the harbour.

Fate 3
Pearl one, knit one.

Fate 2
That unseen dark sea god, with punitive and splintered care.

Fate 1
Turns the ship
With a sweep of his hand
To rock.

Fates 2 *and* **3**
Into a rock.

Fate 2
And the Phaeacians stand and stare
And pine.
And curse their kindness to strangers.
Kill cattle for Poseidon,
Asking his forgiveness for offering passage to
Such dangerous fare.

Fate 3 *cuts a thread of wool.*

Scene Twenty-one

Soundscape – seashore, birds, gulls.

Odysseus *is lying centre stage – face down. He rolls over and awakes, suddenly – as if emerging from a bad dream.*

Odysseus   Where am I now?! What place is this?! They promised to bring me to Ithaca. What soil is this!? They leave me here asleep, no protector, on this alien isle, unthinking friends, liars! Cheats!!

Athene *enters, disguised (badly) as a timid shepherd boy.*

Odysseus   Tell me friend, good shepherd boy. I've been at sea.

Silence.

Washed up on these shores.

Silence.

Washed up, you see.
What island is this? I do not know where I am.

Silence.

I am a simple man, you see, easily confused.

Silence.

What isle is this? Tell me dear friend?
What name is given to this place?

Athene *talks in a ridiculous rural accent.*

Athene   Do you not recognise the coastline, Sir?

Odysseus *shakes his head.*

Athene   The green richness of the land?

Odysseus *shakes his head.*

Athene   The soft breeze that flows from the sea in the morning?

Odysseus   No.

Athene   The olives.

Odysseus   What?

Athene   The olives, do you not recognise the olives, Sir?

Odysseus   Why would I recognise the olives?

Athene   Dunno, you might, Sir.

Odysseus   And when would I have had time to eat any?

Athene   Dunno Sir, you just might. Thems very particular, olives round here.

Odysseus   Tell me the name of this fair isle, friend?

Athene   Don't recognise the sheep then?

Odysseus   Its name?

Athene   Ithaca.

Odysseus   Ithaca. Yes, I have heard of this Ithaca. (*Pause.*) I am from Crete and have many children of all ages that run about that island there, far from here. I am a fugitive.

Athene *addresses him in her normal speaking voice.*

Athene   Stop. Please. Please stop. Even now, even now that you are on your own land, you will not put down your words of cunning and craftiness. And this is why I favoured you, Odysseus, but do not lie to me.

Odysseus   Goddess, forgive me. I did not recognise you.

Athene   Well . . . I was in disguise. Come, there is work to do. The barbarian suitors still devour your home, and insist more aggressively every day Penelope should remarry. You must go into your palace undetected and there forge a plan.

Odysseus   How can they fail to recognise me?

Athene   Go as a beggar. Stand up.

Odysseus *stands.*

Athene   I will age your skin, caress its smooth surface with lines and reckless sun. I will ashen your hair and place darkness beneath your eyes and your chin. And the light in those eyes will diminish, so no one will perceive the courage of Odysseus beneath. I will be close at hand.

Soundscape – knitting.

Athene *and* **Odysseus** *exeunt.*

Scene Twenty-two

Odysseus*'s palace.* **Melantho** *enters, shouting. She is carrying* **Penelope***'s woven cloth.*

Melantho   It is unpicked. It is unpicked!

The **Suitors** *rush in, in response to her shouting.*

Melantho   It is unpicked!

More **Suitors** *enter. She holds the cloth up to show the assembly.*

Melantho   She unpicks it! She unpicks it at night, the 'honourable' Penelope, unpicks her weaving.

Melantho *moves around the* **Suitors** *showing them.* **Antinous** *begins to thud his foot against the floor,* **Eurymachus** *follows his example.*

Melantho   You will wait endlessly for her to agree to marry one of you, because this weaving was never to be finished, the 'honourable' Penelope!

All the **Suitors** *thud their feet in unison on the floor.*

Penelope *and* **Telemachus** *enter, followed by* **Eurycleia** *and* **Penelope's Women**.

Antinous   You must choose, you must choose now. You have tricked us.

Eurymachus   We have waited here with patience, for the day you would choose one of us and make him your husband.

Suitor 1   We have courted and waited and courted and waited here, for your choice.

Suitor 2   You have deceived us.

Suitor 3   You have been unpicking your weaving at night.

Suitor 2   Your cloth was never to be finished.

Telemachus   You are not welcome guests, you are eating and drinking every day, still further into my father's wealth. We have pleaded with you to go, yet you still stay.

Odysseus (*as beggar*) *enters and starts moving among the* **Suitors** *with a begging bowl asking for food.*

Antinous   You must choose, you must choose now. You have tricked us.

Telemachus   Odysseus will return.

Antinous   Telemachus, faithful son, your father is dead. Your mother has deceived these honourable men of Ithaca. Instruct her to choose a husband and the rest of us will leave. It is your own mother's deception that leads you and your household to ruin, not our presence.

Eurymachus   I grieve for you, my lady, it saddens me your loss. He was a great and noble man, but you must accept that he is gone, gone for ever. Choose, choose one of us, you have the best Achaean nobles here. Bring peace and order back to this place.

Silence.

Penelope   I will choose.

Telemachus   No! No, Mother!

Penelope *exits. Her* **Women** *follow;* **Eurycleia** *stays behind, concerned for* **Telemachus**. **Odysseus** *continues around the room, begging.*

Suitor 1   Well said, Eurymachus.

Suitor 2   Well persuaded.

Suitor 3   Well done.

Antinous   Fine words, Brother. Bow, Telemachus, to us here, for your father is amongst us.

The **Suitors** *laugh.* **Eurycleia** *brings* **Telemachus** *a bowl of food and sits with him.*

Eurycleia   Find hope, Sire. Find hope, Telemachus.

Telemachus   Where, old nurse, where can hope be found now?

The **Suitors** *sit, eat and drink.*

Odysseus (*to* **Antinous**)   Spare me a morsel of your food, friend? In my eyes you seem amongst the noblest Achaeans here, not amongst the meanest. If I had wealth such as yours, many gifts I would make to those dispossessed souls such as I. Once I too had servants and houses to ease my life, but I was tempted to travel to Egypt with seemingly good men, but they proved reckless and unruly. Once we had anchored . . .

Antinous   What care I for this? Stand away from my table. Go over there. You know no difference between each of us but stand in front of all with your praises and your storytelling. Stand away.

Odysseus   Oh sad it is to find a man without compassion, with no thoughts for the hungry belly that hounds me into asking. Fate can turn on us so quickly, Antinous.

Antinous   An arrogant beggar too.

Odysseus   And that good looks are not matched by a good heart.

Antinous *hits* **Odysseus**, *who falls. The* **Suitors** *laugh.*

Telemachus   Antinous, this place is a hall for guests. This beggar too is a guest. It is known that gods themselves appear in the most unlikely form and whether or not this beggar is such, he deserves our civility and pity. Sit here, far-travelled man. Eurycleia, get a bowl of food for this man; there is still courtesy in the house of Odysseus.

Eurycleia *does so.* **Penelope** *enters, followed by her* **Women**.

The room falls silent.

Penelope　I will marry the man that can string Odysseus's bow and shoot the arrow through the axes hanging by the door, as Odysseus could. Whatever man can do this feat will be my husband.

The **Suitors** *clap.*

Eurycleia *drops a cup she is offering* **Odysseus**, *looking transfixed at his leg. The noise of the room diminishes for a moment in response to the sound.* **Odysseus** *watches her intently. The chatter of the* **Suitors** *resumes.* **Eurycleia** *walks away.* **Odysseus** *follows her. They speak, unheard by the rest of the assembly.*

Eurycleia (*whispered*)　The scar. The scar from the white bull, you have Odysseus's scar. It is you. I know it is you. I knew you would return. I must run and tell my lady now.

Odysseus　Do you mean to kill me?

Eurycleia　No, my lord, no!

Odysseus　Then you must not utter a word, a word of this to anyone. You understand?

Eurycleia　Of course my lord, of course. I would never betray you. I nursed you, as I nursed your son, I would never betray you.

Odysseus　The suitors would kill me straight if they knew of my presence here. Eurycleia, good friend, when the time has come for Penelope's task, when she asks the suitors to test their strength against the bow, lock all these doors and bring Telemachus to me.

Eurycleia　Yes my lord. Yes.

Odysseus   And take all the weapons out of this hall, say you are taking them away for cleaning. So they have none to grab when their time comes.

Eurycleia   Yes my lord.

Eurycleia *hurriedly kisses* **Odysseus**'s *hand and moves off. Four men enter carrying* **Odysseus**'s *bow.* **Penelope** *goes to leave.*

Antinous   Penelope, will you not stay, will you not watch what prince amongst us is to take your hand?

Penelope   No. I do not intend to watch, Antinous. As you well know, I have no favourites amongst you and therefore I have no interest in observing the winner, or watching the winner's pride.

Penelope *leaves and her* **Women** *follow her.*

Odysseus *nods to* **Eurycleia**. **Eurycleia** *starts closing (locking) the doors. She moves paper screens across the space – enclosing the performance space, so the action cannot be seen by the audience.*

The **Suitors** *relish this competition, whooping and cheering as each one attempts to string the bow – as if watching a weightlifting competition.*

Suitor 1   Let me try first. I'm a good shot. It is heavy. Heavy for any man.

The screens close off all view of the **Suitors**.

Suitor 2   Let me. These muscles are made of iron, my friends, from long nights at sea.

This continues with one man going up after another – to great jeering from the crowd. And 'You can do it', 'You can lift it', 'It's too heavy'. Followed by 'whooping' and 'ahh', and laughter as they fail.
Odysseus *stands outside the room (outside the screens).*
Eurycleia *brings* **Telemachus** *to his side. Dominated by the noise of the* **Suitors** *within,* **Odysseus** *and* **Eurycleia** *clearly tell* **Telemachus** *(inaudible to audience) who* **Odysseus** *is,* **Eurycleia** *showing the scar on his leg.*

Telemachus *does not seem initially to believe and then accepts, hugging his father.* **Telemachus** *and* **Odysseus** *listen to* **Eurymachus** *as he takes the floor (behind the screen) to try the bow.*

Antinous   Eurymachus, my friend, you have strength enough for stringing that bow.

Odysseus *and* **Telemachus** *go inside the room (behind the screens).* **Odysseus** *stops* **Eurycleia** *from joining them and she waits outside — looking through a crack in the screens.*

Eurymachus   I am all words I fear, my brother, more words than strength, Antinous, but I will try my strength for Penelope.

Eurymachus *is able to lift it. 'He's lifting the bow', 'He's lifting it'. But he is not able to string it.*

I can't string it. Antinous, it is now your go. You who have more strength and guile than any amongst us. Come brother, string this bow.

The **Suitors** *cheer as* **Antinous** *approaches the stage to lift the bow. He lifts the bow, almost strings it but fails. Reaction from assembly: 'He cannot do it', 'He cannot do it'.*

Odysseus   Let me try. Antinous, the last of you has failed, let me try.

Antinous   Do not insult us with your impudence, Beggar, you stand amongst princes.

Eurymachus   Stand down.

Telemachus   What harm is there in his trying? My mother will never marry a beggar, let him try since all others have failed. Let him try.

Some of the **Suitors** *cheer and others boo. Some shout out 'Let him try'.*

Telemachus   Let him, what harm is there in that?

Eurycleia *watching from the side of the stage through the gap is joined by* **Melantho**. *Silence.*

Melantho   What's happening, what's happening in there? Eurycleia, why are all the doors shut?

Eurycleia   Shhh. The beggar.

Melantho   That scruff.

Eurycleia   The beggar has picked up the bow. They are silent watching him.

Antinous   Now you've lifted it, try and string it, Beggar.

Silence.

Eurycleia   He's strung the bow. I knew he would. You could see he's noble blood. You could see it. Telemachus stands beside him, now he's drawing the bow right back.

Soundscape of shot of a bow and arrow. **Suitors** *react.*

He's shot through all the axes, right through.

Melantho   Our lady cannot marry a beggar.

Eurycleia   This is no ordinary beggar, Melantho.

Eurymachus   Stand down, Beggar. Give the bow back.

General noise and grumblings from the **Suitors***.*

Melantho   Has he put down the bow?

Eurycleia   No, he's putting another arrow in it. Antinous is looking away, back at his table, eating. The beggar is taking aim.

Sound of arrow going through a neck. **Melantho** *lets out an instinctive scream.*

Suitor 1   Antinous is dead.

Eurymachus   Miserable stranger, are you out of your wits?

Suitor 2   The beggar killed him!

Eurymachus   What man are you?

Scuffling from behind screens. 'The weapons', 'The weapons have gone', 'There are no swords'.

Eurycleia　Telemachus is by his side, fighting next to the beggar.

Sound of a further set of arrows shot across hall.

Suitor 1　Throw the arrows back at him.

Suitor 3　Kill him.

Soundscape – shooting of arrows.

Eurycleia　They fall by his side, the arrows stop short, as if a god was preventing them from reaching him. He picks them up again, Telemachus too.

Soundscape – shooting of arrows.

The suitors fall like flies, like the parasites they were.

General chaos – more blood on screens – arrows shot, shouting from the **Suitors**.

Melantho　He'll kill them all.

Eurycleia　Yes, I believe he will.

Soundscape – shooting of arrows.

Odysseus　I am King Odysseus; this is my palace you have desecrated in your reckless greed. Now take your leave, all of you.

Melantho　Odysseus! Eurymachus, is he still living?

Eurycleia　I cannot see, I cannot see for the mayhem, for the blood.

Melantho　I shall tell the others, all the fathers of those dead men, dead in there.

Melantho *exits, shouting her last line off stage.*

There will be no end to this bloodletting.

Soundscape – noise of **Suitors** *dying reaches its peak. The screens collapse revealing the dead men – face down, flat, on the floor,* **Odysseus** *and* **Telemachus** *the sole survivors.*

Odysseus   Eurycleia, get your mistress.

Soundscape – knitting and **Melantho** *running – as the* **Suitors** *exeunt.*

Fate 1   But Melantho runs across the green, green land, across the dusty paths, to Eurymachus's father, to Alcinous's father and brothers.

Fate 3   Let the warring continue.

Fate 2 *responds to her sisters by knitting faster – and mouthing 'pearl one, knit one' under her breath.*

Fate 1   Let the pain of blood spilling continue in a never-ending Troy.

Fate 3   Let the blood spilt elsewhere, overseas, be carried by Odysseus into his own land, into Ithaca.

Fate 1   And all the young men down, to wander in the Asphodel Fields.

Scene Twenty-three

Penelope *enters, brought in by* **Eurycleia**, *to greet* **Odysseus**.

Telemachus   Mother, your husband has returned. Greet him. (*Pause.*) Why do you stand so distant? Mother?

Eurycleia *touches* **Telemachus***'s hand, beckoning him to leave. Exeunt.* **Penelope** *and* **Odysseus** *are left alone on the stage.*

Penelope   Each moment, woven with longing, in the hope that this day would arrive. I've grown, in suffering, used to the long still note of grief – and many times I asked what delayed my husband? What was so merry elsewhere, once Troy was conquered, that he did not return to me; further suffering the indignities of those suitors, those barbarian men claiming nobility. Many have wandered through this hall since my husband left and I, with a soft heart, heard their stories, and sometimes succumbed to their trickery. And this I fear is one more trick. I look at you and perhaps you could be my Odysseus, my golden man – and then there is such disorder in you, such that I do not recognise my lord and his calm ways, that I miss. There is violence written all over you.

Odysseus   Lady, it is true that peaceful ways have been denied me. Killing ploughs a dark path within; the grasping self left dominant over other selves, and has burnt hard across my gentler ways. Teach me again the loving hand of home, that I may ease the accustomed violence within, and that with our love, the heat of war may finally diminish in my being, and I may die quietly in old age by your side.

Penelope   My bed you shall not share, until I am certain, certain of you. I will sleep in another room, and my bed, which is the most comfortable in this house, we shall move to an adjoining room, there you may lie.

Odysseus (*angry*)   How is that possible? I myself made our marriage bed and one corner of it is made from an olive tree that grows, still thick and twisting from the ground; that bed cannot be moved. Have you changed it?! Have you dismantled our marriage bed so soon?

Penelope   Not so soon, not so soon. It stands as it always has.

Odysseus   You tricked me?

Penelope   Yes, I tricked you. Only you could know how that bed was made, Odysseus, my love.

Commotion. **Fathers** *and* **Brothers** *of the dead* **Suitors** *enter, closely followed by* **Telemachus**.

Father 1   I am the father of Antinous.

Father 2   I am the father of Eurymachus.

Brother 1   And you are outnumbered.

Father 1   With no weapons and only bare hands to protect you and your queen.

They rush him.

Soundscape – thunder. **Athene** *enters.*

Athene   End. Cease. I demand it, by my father's thunderbolt. I demand an end, an end to this unwise, pointless shedding of further blood.

Only those who lack wisdom will continue such warring and my father's thunder will burn you, quicker than the fires of Phlegethon. (*To* **Fathers** *and* **Brothers**.) You men depart and do not bother this household again. Bring peace to your homeland. Your unruly sons showed great disloyalty here, be wiser. (*To* **Odysseus** *and* **Penelope**.) Make an offering to the Earthshaker, Poseidon, Odysseus, and be peaceful.

All exeunt including the **Fates**.

Scene Twenty-four

Soundscape – birdsong.

Laertes *enters, frail and elderly. One by one and with great difficulty (back aching each time he stretches up again), he brings in three small fruit trees in pots. Once they are all in place, he puts on a pair of glasses, takes out a pair of secateurs, and prunes.* **Odysseus** *enters and watches for some time* **Laertes** *going about his business, mumbling to himself.*

Odysseus   Old friend, your garden is kept well.

Laertes   Oh! Oh yes, yes. So it is.

Laertes *squints as he attempts to focus on* **Odysseus** *and then continues pruning.*

Odysseus   I'm a visitor to these parts. Once when I was in my native country a man came to the gates claiming to be from Ithaca, son to Laertes. He was a man of great character. He entertained us for many nights with his stories of Troy.

Laertes *has stopped pruning.*

Laertes   Stranger, it is my son you entertained, parted from us now for many years, dead we believe.

His mother walks with the Shades, her heart could no longer live without the needed presence of her son; life simply fell away from that most gracious woman. Forgive my attire, I am dishevelled, I know. The will for life departed many years ago, when he left. Tell me, how was my son? How many years ago did you meet him?

Odysseus   I will tell you truthfully, I am the son of Prince Apheidas; we live to the north of here, a peaceful island it is, with good people. It is some four years since I met Odysseus, unhappy man; he was making his way here when I saw him last.

Laertes *interrupts* **Odysseus**.

Laertes (*with sadness*)   My son.

He turns away and goes back to his pruning.

My son.

Odysseus *watches and then speaks.*

Odysseus   I am the one you seek. Dry your eyes. I'm the one. See, here is the scar, the wound I received, many years past, from the white boar's tusk. How I cried. Father.

He wanders around the trees, trying to choose one.

And these trees, now one you gave to me. I remember as a child following you about the place. I wanted my own tree and you in tolerance gave me one, one of these fine bushes. This one, this one is mine, I think.

Laertes   Odysseus. Odysseus, you are home.

Odysseus *takes* **Laertes**'*s secateurs and starts pruning.*

Odysseus   Here, let me help you.

Laertes *watches his son as he prunes his tree. Lights dim.*

Fate 1 *enters and walks to the end space, sits and knits. Once she is seated* **Fate 2** *does likewise, filling the next space to her, followed by* **Fate 3**. *Soundscape – knitting. All the female performers enter, quickly filling the space, and sit and knit, looking down at their knitting. Once all the spaces are filled and the soundscape of knitting reaches a climax, all the women, in unison, look up at the audience. Black out.*